T H E

CHAMPION OF VIRTUE.

A

GOTHIC STORY.

By the EDITOR of the PHŒNIX;

A TRANSLATION OF

BARCLAY'S ARGENIS.

Ficta voluptatis caufâ fint proxima veris.

HORACE.

PRINTED for the AUTHOR,

By W. KEYMER, Colchefter, and fold by him;
Sold alfo by G. ROBINSON, No. 25, Pater-
nofter-Row, London.

M.LCC.LXXVII.

THE

CHAMPION

OF

VIRTUE

[PRICE THREE SHILLINGS.]

ADDRESS

READER.

READER, before you enter upon the hiftory before you, permit the Author to hold a fhort conference with you, upon certain points that will elucidate the defign, and perhaps induce you to form a *favourable*, as well as a right judgment of the work.

Pray did you ever read a book called, The Caftle of Otranto? if you have, you will willingly enter with me into a review of it.—but perhaps you have not read it? however you have heard

A   that

that it is an attempt to blend together, the moſt attractive and intereſting cir-cumſtances of the ancient romance and modern Novel; but poſſibly you may not know ſo much, *ſtill* you have read *ſome* ancient Romance, or *ſome* modern Novel, it will be ſtrange if you have not in this age !

But ſuppoſe you ſhould diſlike or deſ-piſe them both ? 'tis no matter ! I ſhall catch you ſome way or other.

You delight in the fables of the anci-ents, the old poets, or ſtory-tellers.

Or, you are pleaſed with the won-derful adventures of modern travellers, ſuch as Gaudentio di Lucca, or Robinſon Cruſoe.

Or, if you are unacquainted with any of the books already mentioned, I would venture a good wager that you have read the Pilgrim's Progreſs.

You ſmile ! but I mean nothing ludi-crous, the Pilgrim's Progreſs is a work of genius, and as ſuch I reſpect it.—is it poſſible that a book merely fanatical, ſhould have run through fifty-four edi-tions ? you may ſafely conclude it has

merit

merit of a higher kind, that enables it to blunt the shafts of ridicule, and to stand its ground, notwithstanding the variations of times and tastes, and the refinements of literature and language.

But what (say you) is all this to the purpose? patience a moment, and I will come directly to the point.—if you have read any *fictitious* or *fabulous* story, it will answer my intention; which is to assert, that all readers, of all times and countries have delighted in stories of these kinds ; and that those who affect to despise them under one form, will receive and embrace them in another.

History represents human nature as it is.—alas ! too often a melancholy retrospect.—romance displays only the amiable side of the picture ; it shows the pleasing features, and throws a veil over the blemishes: mankind are naturally pleased with what gratifies their vanity, and vanity like all other passions of the human heart, may be rendered subservient to good and useful purposes.

I confess that it may be abused, and become an instrument to corrupt the

A 2   manners

manners and morals of mankind ; fo may poetry, fo may plays, fo may every kind of compofition ; but that will prove nothing more than the old faying lately revived'——" that every earthly thing has two handles."

The bufinefs of romance is firft to excite the attention, and fecondly to direct it to fome ufeful, or at leaft innocent end. Happy the writer who attains both thefe points, like Richardfon ! and not unfortunate, or undeferving of praife, he who gains only the latter, and furnifhes out of it an entertainment for the reader !

Having, in fome degree, opened my defign, I beg leave to conduct my reader back again, till he comes within view of the caftle of Otranto ; a work which has already been obferved, is an attempt to unite the various merits and graces of the ancient romance and modern Novel.---to attain this end, there is required a fufficient degree of the marvellous to excite the attention.—— enough of the manners of real life, to give an air of probability to the work ;---
and

and enough of the pathetic to engage the heart in its behalf.

The book before us is excellent in the two last points, but has a redundancy in the first; the opening excites the attention very strongly; the conduct of the story is artful and judicious; the characters are admirably drawn and supported; the diction polished and elegant; yet with all these brilliant advantages, it palls upon the mind, though it does not upon the ear, and the reason is obvious; the machinery is so violent, that it destroys the effect it is intended to excite. Had the story been kept within the utmost *verge* of probability, the effect had been preserved, without losing the least circumstance that excites or detains the attention.

For instance, we can conceive and allow of the appearance of a ghost, we can even dispense with an enchanted sword and helmet, but then they must keep within certain limits of credibility, a sword so large as to require an hundred men to lift it, a helmet that by its own weight forces a passage through a

court-

court-yard into an arched vault, big enough for a man to go through; a picture that walks out of its frame; a skeleton ghoft in a hermit's cowl: when your expectation is wound up to the highest pitch, these circumstances take it down with a witness, deftroy the work of imagination, and instead of attention, excite laughter. I was both surprised and vexed to find the enchantment diffolved, that I wished might continue to the end of the book, and several others of its readers have confeffed the fame disappointment to me; the beauties are so numerous, that we cannot bear the defects, but want it to be perfect in all respects.

In the course of my obfervations upon this fingular book, it feemed to me that it was poffible to compofe a work upon the fame plan, wherein thefe defects might be avoided, and the *keeping* as in *painting* might be preferved.

But then, faid I, it might happen to the writer as it has to the imitators of Shakefpeare, the *unities* may be preferved,

ferved, but the *fpirit* may evaporate; in fhort it will be fafeft to let it alone.

During thefe reflections, it occured to my remembrance, that a certain friend of mine was in poffeffion of a manufcript in the old Englifh language, containing a ftory that anfwered in almoft every point to the plan above-mentioned; and if it were modernifed, might afford entertainment to thofe who delight in ftories of this kind.

Accordingly (with my friend's per-miffion) I tranfcribed, or rather tranf-lated a few fheets of it.---I read it to a circle of friends of approved judgment, they gave me the warmeft encourage-ment to proceed, and even made me promife to finifh it.

Here it is, therefore, at your fervice; if you are pleafed, I am fatisfied; I will venture to affure you that it fhall not leave you worfe than it finds you in any refpect. If you defpife the work it will go to fleep quietly with many of its contemporaries, and the *ghoft of it* will not difturb your repofe.

I am, with profound Refpect,
Reader, your moft obedient Servant,
The EDITOR.

CHAMPION of VIRTUE.

A

GOTHIC STORY.

IN the minority of Henry the Sixth, king of England, who alſo was crowned king of France, when the renowned John duke of Bedford was regent of France, and Humphrey the good duke of Gloucester was protector of England; a worthy knight, called ſir Philip Harclay, returned from his travels, to England, his native country.—He had ſerved under the glorious king Henry the Fifth with diſtinguiſhing valour, had acquired an honourable fame, and was no leſs eſteemed for chriſtian virtues than for deeds of chivalry. After the death of his prince, he entered into the ſervice of the Greek emperor, and diſtinguiſhed his courage againſt the encroachments of the Saracens. In a battle there, he took priſoner a certain gentleman, by name M. Zadiſky, of Greek extraction, but brought up by a Saracen officer, this man he converted to the chriſtian faith, after which he bound him to himſelf by the tyes of friendſhip and gratitude, and he reſolved to continue with his benefactor. After

B thirty

thirty years travel and warlike fervice, he determined to return to his native land, and to spend the remainder of his life in peace, and by devoting himfelf to works of piety and charity, prepare for a better ftate hereafter. This noble knight had in his early youth contracted a ftrict friendfhip with the only fon of the lord Lovel, a gentleman of eminent virtues and accomplifhments. During fir Philip's refidence in foreign countries, he had frequently written to his friend, and had for a time received anfwers, the laft informed him of the death of the old lord Lovel, and the marriage of the young one; but from that time he heard no more from him. Sir Philip imputed it not to neglect or forgetfulnefs, but to the difficulties of intercourfe, common at that time to all travellers and adventurers.— When he was returning home, he refolved, after looking into his family affairs, to vifit the caftle of Lovel, and enquire into the fituation of his friend.—He landed in Kent, attended by his Greek friend and two faithful fervants, one of which was maimed by the wounds he had received in the defence of his mafter.—Sir Philip went to his family feat in Yorkfhire, he found his mother and fifter were dead, and his eftates fequeftered in the hands of commiffioners appointed by the protector.—He was obliged to prove the reallity of his claim, and the identity of his perfon, (by the teftimony of fome of the old fervants of his family) after which every thing was reftored to him. He took poffeffion of his own houfe, eftablifhed his houfehold, fettled the old fervants in their former ftations, and placed thofe he brought home in
the

the upper offices of his family. He left his friend to fuperintend his domeftic affairs, and attended by only one of his old fervants, he fet out for the caftle of Lovel, in the weft of England.—They travelled by eafy journeys, but towards the evening of the fecond day, the fervant was fo ill and fatigued he could go no further, he ftopped at an inn where he grew worfe every hour, and the next day expired. Sir Philip was under great concern for the lofs of his fervant, and fome for himfelf, being a-lone in a ftrange place; however he took cou-rage, ordered his fervant's funeral, attended it himfelf, and having fhed a tear of humanity over his grave, proceeded alone on his journey. As he drew near the eftate of his friend, he began to enquire of every one he met, whe-ther the lord Lovel refided at the feat of his anceftors; he was anfwered by or.e, he did not know,—by another he could not tell,—by a third, that he never heard of fuch a perfon. Sir Philip thought it ftrange that a man of lord Lovel's confequence fhould be unknown in his own neighbourhood, and where his anceftors had ufually refided.—He ruminated on the un-certainty of human happinefs; this world, faid he, has nothing for a wife man to depend upon, I have loft all my relations and moft of my friends, and I am uncertain whether any are remaining.—I will however be thankful for the bleffings that are fpared to me, and I will endeavour to replace thofe that I have loft.— if my friend lives he fhall fhare my fortune while I live, and his children fhall have the re-verfion of it, and I will fhare his comforts in re-turn.—But perhaps my friend may have met

with

with troubles that have made him difgufted with the world. Perhaps he has buried his amiable wife, or his promifing children, and tired of public life, he is retired into a monaftry,—at leaft I will know what all this filence means.

When he came within a mile of the caftle of Lovel, he ftopped at a cottage, and afked for a draught of water, a peafant, mafter of the houfe brought it, and afked if his honour would alight and take a moments refrefhment.—Sir Philip accepted his offer, being refolved to make farther enquiry before he approached the caftle.—He afked the fame queftions of him, that he had before to others, which lord Lovel, faid the man, does your honour enquire after? the man whom I knew, was called Arthur, faid fir Philp, ay, faid the peafant, he was the only furviving fon of Richard lord Lovel as I think?—very true friend, he was fo.—alas fir, faid the man, he is dead! he furvived his father but a fhort time.—dead fay you.—how long fince?—about fifteen years to the beft of my remembrance.—fir Philip fighed deeply—alas, faid he, what do we by living long, but furvive all our friends!—but pray tell me how he died.—I will fir to the beft of my knowledge. An't pleafe your honour, I heard fay, that he attended the king when he went againft the Welch rebels, and he left his lady big with child; and fo there was a battle fought, and the king got the better of the rebels,—there came firft a report that none of the officers were killed, but a few days after there came a meffenger with an account very different, that feveral were wounded, and that the lord Lovel was flain, which fad news overfet us all with forrow,

forrow, for he was a noble gentleman, a bountiful mafter, and the delight of all the neighbourhood.—He was indeed, faid fir Philip, all that is amiable and good, he was my dear and noble friend, and I am inconfolable for his lofs.—but the unfortunate lady, what became of her? why an't pleafe your honour, they faid fhe died of grief for the lofs of her hufband, but her death was kept private for a time, and we did not know it for certain till fome weeks afterwards—The will of heaven be obeyed, faid fir Philip, but who fucceeded to the title and eftate? the next heir, faid the peafant, a kinfman of the deceafed, fir Walter Lovel by name. I have feen him, faid fir Philip, formerly, but where was he when thefe events happened? at the caftle of Lovel, fir. he came there on a vifit to the lady, and waited there to receive my lord, at his return from Wales, when the nesws of his death arrived, fir Walter did every thing in his power to comfort her, and fome faid he was to marry her, but fhe refufed to be comforted, and took it fo to heart that fhe died. And does the prefent lord Lovel refide at the caftle?—no fir,—who then?—the lord baron Fitz-Owen.—and how came fir Walter to leave the feat of his anceftors?—why fir e married his fifter to this faid lord, and fo he fold the caftle to him, and went away, and built himfelf a houfe in the north country, as far as Northumberland, I think they call it. That is very ftrange, faid fir Philip,—fo it is pleafe your honour, but this is all I know about it— I thank you friend for your intelligence, I have taken a long journey to no purpofe, and have met with nothing but crofs accidents.—This

life

life is indeed a pilgrimage,—pray direct me the
neareſt way to the next monaſtry,—noble ſir,
ſaid the peaſant, it is full five miles off, the
night is coming on, and the ways are bad; I
am but a poor man and cannot entertain your
honour as you are uſed to, but if you will enter
my poor cottage, that, and every thing in it
are at your ſervice. My honeſt friend I thank
you heartily, ſaid ſir Philip, your kindneſs and
hoſpitality might ſhame many of higher birth
and breeding, I will accept your kind offer;
but pray let me know the name of my hoſt?—
John Wyat, ſir, an honeſt man though a poor
one, and a chriſtian man, though a ſinful one,
Whoſe cottage is this?—it belongs to the lord
Fitz-Owen.—what family have you?—a wife,
two ſons and a daughter, who will all be proud
to wait upon your honour; let me hold your
honour's ſtirrup whilſt you alight. He ſeconded
theſe words by the proper action, and having
aſſiſted his gueſt to diſmount, he conducted him
into his houſe, called his wife to attend him,
and then led his horſe under a poor ſhed, that
ſerved him as a ſtable. Sir Philip was fatigued in body and mind, and was glad to repoſe himſelf any where. The courteſy of his
hoſt engaged his attention, and ſatisfied his
wiſhes. He ſoon after returned, followed by
a youth of about eighteen years, make haſte
John, ſaid the father, and before you ſay neither more nor leſs than what I have told you.
I will father, ſaid the lad, and immediately ſet
off, run like a buck acroſs the fields, and was
out of ſight in an inſtant. I hope friend, ſaid
ſir Philip, you have not ſent your ſon to provide for my entertainment, I am a ſoldier, uſed

to lodge and fare hard, and if it were otherwife, your courtefy and kindnefs would give a
relifh to the moft ordinary food. I wifh
heartily, faid Wyatt, it was in my power to
entertain your honour as you ought to be, but
as I cannot do fo, I will, when my fon returns
acquaint you with the errand I fent him on.
After this they converfed together on common
fubjects, like fellow creatures of the fame natural form and endowments, tho' different kinds
of education had given a confcious fuperiority
to the one, a confcious inferiority to the other;
and the due refpect was paid by the latter, without being exacted by the former.—In about
half an hour young John returned—thou haft
made hafte, faid the father; not more than
good fpeed, quoth the fon—tell us then how
you fped?—fhall I tell all that paffed, faid
John?—all, faid the father, I dont want to
hide any thing. John ftood with his cap in
his hand, and thus told his tale.—I went ftraight
to the caftle as faft as I could run, it was my
hap to light on young mafter Edmund firft, fo
I told him juft as you bad me, that a noble
gentleman was come a long journey from foreign parts to fee the lord Lovel, his friend,
and having lived abroad many years, he did
not know that he was dead, and that the caftle was fallen into other hands; that upon
hearing thefe tidings he was much grieved and
difappointed, and wanting a night's lodging
to reft himfelf before he returned to his own
home, he was fain to take up with one at our
cottage; that my father thought my lord would
be angry with him, if he were not told of the
ftranger's journey and intentions, efpecially to
let

let fuch a man lye at our cottage, where he could neither be lodged nor entertained according to his quality. Here John ftopped, and his father exclaimed, a good lad?—you did your errand very well; and tell us the anfwer—John proceeded—mafter Edmund ordered me fome beer, and went to acquaint my lord of the meffage, he ftayed a while, and then came back to me. John, faid he, tell the noble ftranger, that the baron Fitz-Owen greets him well, and defires him to reft affured, that though lord Lovel is dead, and the caftle fallen into other hands, his friends will always find a welcome there; and my lord defires that he will accept of a lodging there, while he remains in this country—fo I come away directly, and made hafte to deliver my errand.

Sir Philip expreffed fome difatisfaction at this mark of old Wyatt's refpect—I wifh, faid he, that you had acquainted me with your intention before you fent to inform the baron I was here. I choofe rather to lodge with you, and I propofe to make amends for the trouble I fhall give you. Pray fir dont mention it, faid the peafant, you are as welcome as myfelf, I hope no offence; the only reafon of my fending was, becaufe I am both unable and unworthy to entertain your honour.—I am forry, faid fir Philip, you fhould think me fo dainty, I am a chriftian foldier, and him I acknowledge for my prince and mafter, accepted the invitations of the poor, and wafhed the feet of his difciples. Let us fay no more on this head, I am refolved to ftay this night in your cottage, tomorrow I will wait on the baron, and thank him for his hofpitable invitation.—That fhall be

be as your honour pleafes, fince you will condefcend to ftay here. John, do you run back
and acquaint my lord of it; not fo, faid fir
Philip, it is now almoft dark,—'tis no matter,
faid John, I can go it blindfold. Sir Philip
then gave him a meffage to the baron in his
own name, acquainting him that he would pay
his refpects to him in the morning. John flew
back the fecond time, and foon returned with
new commendations from the baron, and that
he would expect him on the morrow. Sir
Philip gave him an angel of gold, and praifed
his fpeed and abilities.

He fupped with Wyatt and his family upon
new laid eggs and rafhers of bacon, with the
higheft relifh. They praifed the Creator for
his gifts, and acknowledged they were unworthy of the leaft of his bleffings. They gave
the beft of their two lofts up to fir Philip, the
reft of the family flept in the other, the old
woman and her daughter in the bed, the father and his two fons upon clean ftraw. fir
Philip's bed was of a better kind, and yet as
much inferior to his ufual accommodations;
neverthelefs the good knight flept as well in
Wyatt's cottage, as he could have done in a
palace. During his fleep, many ftrange and
incoherent dreams arofe to his imagination.
He thought he received a meffage from his
friend lord Lovel, to come to him at the caftle,
that he ftood at the gate and received him, that
he ftrove to embrace him, but could not, but
that he fpoke to this effect.—Though I have
been dead thefe fifteen years, I ftill command
here, and none can come here without my permiffion, know that it is I that invite, and bid
you

you welcome, the hopes of my houfe reft upon you. Upon this he bid fir Philip follow him, he led him through many rooms, till at laft he funk down, and fir Philip thought he ftill followed him, till he came into a dark and frightful cave, where he difappeared, and in his ftead he beheld a compleat fuit of armour ftained with blood, which belonged to his friend, and he thought he heard difmal groans from beneath. Prefently after, he thought he was hurried away by an invifible hand, and led into a wild heath, where the people were inclofing the ground, and making preparations for two combatants; the trumpet founded, and a voice called out ftill louder, forbear!—it is not permitted to be revealed till the time is ripe for the event.—Wait with patience on the decrees of heaven—He was then tranfporred to his own houfe, where going into an unfrequented room he was again met by his friend, who was living, and in all the bloom of youth, as when he firft knew him. He ftarted at the fight and awoke. The fun fhone upon his curtains, and perceiving it was day, he fat up and recollected where he was. The images that imprefled his fleeping fancy remained ftrongly on his mind waking; but his reafon ftrove to difperfe them; it was natural that the ftory he had heard fhould create thefe ideas, that they fhould wait on him in his fleep, and that every dream fhould bear fome relation to his deceafed friend. The fun dazzled his eyes, the birds ferenaded him and diverted his attention, and a woodbine forced its way through the window, and regaled his fenfe of fmelling with its fragrance.—He arofe, paid his devotions to

heaven,

heaven, and then carefully defcended the narrow ftairs, and went out at the door of the cottage.—There he faw the induftrious wife and daughter of old Wyatt at their morning work, the one milking her cow, the other feeding her poultry. He afked for a draught of milk, which, with a flice of rye bread, ferved to break his faft. He walked about the fields alone, for old Wyatt and his two fons were gone out to their daily labour. He was foon called back by the good woman, who told him that a fervant from the baron waited to conduct him to the caftle. He took leave of Wyatt's wife, telling her he would fee her again before he left the country. The daughter fetched his horfe, which he mounted, and fet forward with the fervant, of whom he afked many queftions concerning his mafter's family. How long have you lived with the baron?—Ten years.—Is he a good mafter?—Yes fir, and alfo a good hufband and father.—What family has he?—Three fons and a daughter.—What age are they of?—the eldeft fon is in his feventeenth year, the fecond in his fixteenth, the others feveral years younger; but befides thefe my lord has feveral young gentlemen brought up with his own fons, two of which are his nephews; he keeps in his houfe a learned clerk to teach them languages; and as for all bodily exercifes, none come near them; there is a fletcher to teach them the ufe of the crofs bow; a mafter to teach them to ride; another the ufe of the fword; another learns them to dance; and then they wreftle and run, and have fuch activity in all their motions, that it does one good to fee them; and my lord thinks

nothing

nothing too much to beſtow on their education. Truly, ſays ſir Philip, he does the part
of a good parent, and I honour him greatly
for it ; but are the young gentlemen of a promiſing diſpoſition ?—yes indeed ſir, anſwered
the ſervant, the young gentlemen, my lord's
ſons are hopeful youths, but yet there is one
who is thought to exceed them all, though he
is the ſon of a poor labourer..—And who is he,
ſaid the knight? one Edmund Twyford, the
ſon of a cottager in our village, he is to be
ſure as fine a youth as ever the ſun ſhone upon,
and of ſo ſweet a diſpotion that nobody envies
his good fortune.—What good fortune does he
enjoy ?—why ſir about two years ago, my lord,
at his ſons requeſt, took him into his own family, and gives him the ſame education as his
own children ; the young lords doat upon
him, eſpecially maſter William, who is about
his own age. It is ſuppoſed they he will attend
the young lords when they go to the wars,
which my lord intends they ſhall bye and bye.
What you tell me, ſaid ſir Philip, increaſes
every minute my reſpect for your lord, he is
an excellent father and maſter, he ſeeks out
merit in obſcurity, he diſtinguiſhes and rewards
it ; I honour him with all my heart. In this
manner they converſed together till they came
within view of the caſtle. In a field near the
houſe they ſaw a company of youths with croſs
bows in their hands, ſhooting at a mark. There
ſaid the ſervant, are our young gentlemen at
their exerciſes. Sir Philip ſtopped his horſe
to obſerve them, he heard two or three of
them cry out—Edmund is the victor—he wins
the prize ! I muſt, ſaid ſir Philip, take a view
of

of this Edmund—he jumped off his horfe, gave the bridle to the fervant, and walked into the field.—The young gentlemen came up, and paid their refpects to him, he apologized for intruding upon their fports, and afked which was the victor, upon which the youth he fpoke to, beckoned to another, who immediately advanced, and made his obeifance,—as he drew near, fir Philip fixed his eyes upon him, with fo much attention, that he feemed not to obferve his courtefy and addrefs.—at length he recollected himfelf, and faid, what is your name young man ? Edmund Twyford, replied the youth, and I have the honour to attend upon the lord Fitz-Owen's fons.—pray noble fir, faid the youth who firft addreffed fir Philip, are not you the ftranger who is expected by my father ?—I am fir, anfwered he, and I go to pay my refpects to him—will you excufe our attendance fir, we have not yet finifhed our exercifes—my dear youth, faid fir Philip, no apology is neceffary, but will you favour me with your proper name, that I may know to whofe courtefy I am obliged—my name is William Fitz-Owen, that gentleman is my eldeft brother, mafter Robert, that other my kinfman, mafter Richard Wenlock—very well, I thank you gentle fir, I beg you not to ftir another ftep, your fervant holds my horfe, farewel fir, faid mafter William, I hope we fhall have the pleafure of meeting you at din-net—the youths returned to their fports, and fir Philip mounted his horfe and proceeded to the caftle ; he entered it with a deep figh and melancholy recollections. The baron received him with the utmoft refpect and courtefy——

C

he

he gave a brief account of the principal events that had happened in the family of Lovel during his abfence;—he fpoke of the late lord Lovel with refpect, of the prefent with the affection of a brother.—Sir Philip in return gave a brief recital of his own adventures abroad, and of the difagreeable circumftances he had met with fince his return home: he pathetically lamented the lofs of all his friends, not forgetting that of his faithful fervant on the way; faying he could be contented to give up the world, and retire to a religious houfe, but that he was withheld by the confideration, that fome who depended entirely upon him, wou'd want his prefence and affiftance, and befide that, he thought he might be of fervice to many others. The baron agreed with him in opinion, that a man was of much more fervice to the world who continued in it, than one who retired from it, and gave his fortunes to the church, whofe fervants did not always make the beft ufe of it.—Sir Philip then turned the converfation, and congratulated the baron on his hopeful family—he praifed their perfons and addrefs, and warmly applauded the care he beftowed on their education. He liftened with pleafure to the honeft approbation of a worthy heart, and enjoyed the true happinefs of a parent—fir Philip then made further enquiry concerning Edmund, whofe appearance had ftruck him with an impreffion in his favour. That boy, faid the Baron, is the fon of a cottager in this neighbourhood, his uncommon merit and gentlenefs of manners, diftinguifhes him from thofe of his own clafs; from his childhood he attracted the notice and affec-

tion

tion of all that knew him, he was beloved every where but at his father's houfe, and there it fhould feem that his merits were his crimes; for the peafant his father hated him, treated him feverely, and at length threatened to turn him out of doors—he uſed to run here and there on errands for my people, and at length they obliged me to take notice of him; my fons earneftly defired I would take him into my family, I did fo about two years ago, intending to make him their fervant, but his extraordinary genius and difpofition has obliged me to look upon him in a fuperior light; perhaps I may incur the cenfure of many people, by giving him fo many advantages, and treating him as the companion of my children;— his merit muft juſtify or condemn my partiallity for him, however I truft that I have fecured to my children a faithful fervant of the upper kind, and an ufeful friend to my family. Sir Philip warmly applauded his generous hoft, and wifhed to be a fharer in his bounty to that fine youth, whoſe appearance indicated all the qualities that had indeared him to his companions.

At the hour of dinner the young men prefented themfelves before their lord and his gueft— fir Philip addreffed himfelf to Edmund, he afked him many queftions, and received modeft and intelligent anfwers, and he grew every minute more pleafed with him. After dinner the youths withdrew with their tutor to perfue their ftudies—fir Philip fat for fome time, wrapt up in meditation. After fome minutes, the baron afked him if he might not be favoured with the fruits of his contemplations—you fhall my lord, anfwered he, for you have a right to

them

them—I was thinking that when many bleſ-
fings are loſt, we ſhould cheriſh thoſe that remain, and even endeavour to replace the
others—my lord, I have taken a ſtrong liking
to that youth whom you call Edmund Twyford,
—I have neither children nor relations to claim
my fortune, nor ſhare my affections—your
lordſhip has many demands upon your generoſity—I can provide for this promiſing youth
without doing injuſtice to any one, will you
give him to me? he is a fortunate boy, ſaid
the baron, to gain your favour ſo ſoon. My
lord, ſaid the knight, I will confeſs to you, that
the firſt thing that touched my heart in his favour, is a ſtrong reſemblance he bears to a certain dear friend I once had, and his manner
reſembles him as much as his perſon; his qualities deſerve that he ſhould be placed in a
higher rank, I will adopt him for my ſon, and
introduce him into the world as my relation,
if you will reſign him to me, what ſay you?—
ſir, ſaid the baron, you have made a noble
offer, and I am too much the young man's
friend to be a hindrance to his preferment—it
is true that I had intended to provide for him
in my own family, but I cannot do it ſo effectually as by giving him to you, whoſe generous affection being unlimited by other tyes,
may in time perfer him to a higher ſtation as
he ſhall deſerve it—I have only one condition
to make, that the lad ſhall have his option, for
I would not oblige him to leave my ſervice
againſt his inclination.—you ſay well, replied
ſir Philip, nor would I take him upon other
terms—agreed then, ſaid the baron, let us ſend
for Edmund hither. A ſervant was ſent to
fetch

fetch him, he came immediately, and his lor
thus befpoke him—Edmund you own eternal
obligations to this gentleman, who perceiving
in you a certain refemblance to a friend of his,
and liking your behaviour, has taken a great
affection for you, infomuch that he defires
to receive you into his family—I cannot better
provide for you than by difpofing of you to
him, and if you have no objection you fhall
return home with him, when he goes from
hence. The countenance of Edmund under-
went many alterations during this propofal
of his lord, it expreffed tendernefs, gratitude,
and forrow, but the laft was predominant,—
he bowed refpectfully to the baron and fir
Philip, and after fome hefitation fpoke as follows—I feel very ftrongly the obligations I
owe to this gentleman, for his noble and generous offer—I cannot exprefs the fenfe I have of
his goodnefs to me, a peafant boy, only known
to him by my lord's kind and partial mention—
this uncommon bounty claims my eternal gratitude. To you my honoured lord, I owe every
thing, even this gentleman's good opinion—you
diftinguifhed me when nobody elfe did, and next
to you, your fons are my beft and deareft benefactors, they introduced me to your notice.
My heart is unalterably attached to this houfe
and family, and my utmoft ambition is to
fpend my life in your fervice—but if you have
perceived any great and grievous faults in me,
that make you wifh to put me out of your
family, and if you have recommended me to
this gentleman in order to be rid of me, in
that cafe I will fubmit to your pleafure. as I
would if you fhould fentence me to death.——

C 3.   During

During this speech the tears made themse'ves channels down Edmund's cheeks, ard his two noble auditors catching the tender infection, wiped their eyes at the conclusion. My dear child, said the baron, you overcome me by your tenderness and gratitude—I know of no faults you have committed, that I should wish to be rid of you—I thought to do you the best service by promoting you to that of sir Philip Harclay, who is both able and willing to provide for you, but if you prefer my service to his, I will not part with you. Upon this Edmund kneeled to the baron, he embraced his knees--my dear lord, I am and will be your servant, in preference to any man living, I only ask your permission to live and die in your service—you see sir Philip, said the baron, how this boy engages the heart; how can I part with him? I cannot ask you any more, answered sir Philip, I see it is impossible, but I esteem you both still higher than ever, the youth for his gratitude, and your lordship for your noble mind and true generosity, blessings attend you both! Oh sir, said Edmund, pressing the hand of sir Philip, do not think me ungrateful to you, I will ever remember your goodness, and pray to heaven to reward it——the name of sir Philip Harclay shall be engraven upon my heart, next to my lord, and his family for ever. Sir Philip raised the youth and embraced him, saying, if ever you want a friend, remember me, and depend upon my protection, so long as you continue to deserve it. Edmund bowed low and withdrew with his eyes full of tears of sensibility and gratitude.—— When he was gone, sir Philp said, I am thinking

ing that tho' young Edmund wants not my af-
fiitance at prefent, he may hereafter ftand in
need of my friendfhip. I fhould not wonder
if fuch rare qualities as he poffeffes, fhould one
day create envy, and raife him enemies, in
which cafe he might come to lofe your favour,
without any fault of yours or his own. I am
obliged to you for the warning, faid the baron,
I hope it will be unneceffary, but if ever I part
with Edmund, you fhall have the refufal of him.
I thank your lordfhip for all your civilities to
me, I leave my beft wifhes with you and your
hopeful family, and I humbly take my leave.
Will you not ftay one night in the caftle?
faid my lord, you fhall be as welcome a gueft
as ever.—I acknowledge your goodnefs and
hofpitality, but this houfe fills me with melancholy recollections, I came hither with a heavy
heart, and it will not be lighter while I remain
here.—I fhall always remember your lordfhip
with the higheft refpect and efteem, and I pray
God to preferve you, and increafe your bleffings!

After fome further ceremonies, fir Philip
departed, and returned to old Wyatt's, ruminating on the viciffitude of human affairs,
and thinking on the changes he had feen!—

At his return to Wyatt's cottage, he found
the family affembled together—he told them he
would take another night's lodging there,
which they heard with great pleafure, for he
had familiarifed himfelf to them in the laft
evenings converfation, infomuch that they began to enjoy his company—he told Wyatt of
the misfortune he had fuftained by lofing his
fervant on the way, and wifhed he could get
one to attend him home in his place—young
John

John looked earneftly at his father, he returned a look of approbation. I perceive one in this company, faid he, that would be proud to ferve your honour; but I fear he is not brought up well enough.—John coloured with impatience, he could not forbear fpeaking. Sir I can anfwer for an honeft heart, a willing mind, and a light pair of heels, and though I am fomewhat aukward, I fhall be proud to learn, to pleafe my noble mafter, if he will but try me. You fay well, faid fir Philip, I have obferved your qualifications, and if you are defirous to ferve me, I am equally pleafed with you, if your father has no objection I will take you—objection fir, faid the the old man! it will be my pride to prefer him to fuch a noble gentleman. I will make no terms for him, but leave it to your honour, to do for him as he fhall deferve. Very well, faid fir Philip, you fhall be no lofer by that, I will charge myfelf with the care of the young man. The bargain was ftruck, and fir Philip purchafed a horfe for John of the old man. The next morning they fet out, the knight left marks of his bounty with the good couple and departed laden with their bleffing and prayers. He ftopped at the place where his good fervant was buried, and caufed maffes to be faid for the repofe of his foul, went home by eafy journeys, without meeting any thing remarkable by the way—his family rejoiced at his return, he fettled his new fervant in attendance upon his perfon, he then looked round his neighbourhood for objects of his charity— when he faw merit in diftrefs, it was his delight to raife and fupport it—he fpent his

time

time in the service of his Creator, and glorified him in doing good to his creatures——he reflected frequently upon every thing that had befallen him in his late journey to the west, and at his leisure took down all the particulars in writing.

Hear follows an interval of four years, as by the manuscript, this omission seems intended by the writer.

ABOUT

ABOUT this time the prognofticks of fir Philip Harclay began to be verified, that Edmund's good qualities might one day excite envy and create him enemies—the fons and kinfmen of his patron began to feek occafion to find fault with him, and to depreciate him with others—the baron's eldeft fon and heir, mafter Robert, had feveral contefts with mafter William the fecond fon upon his account. This youth had a warm affection for Edmund, and whenever his brother and kinfmen treated him flightly, he fupported him againft their malicious infinuations. Mr. Richard Wenlock and John Markham were the fifters fons of the lord Fitz-Owen, and there were feveral other more diftant relations, who with them fecretly envied Edmund's fine qualities, and ftrove to leffen him in the efteem of the baron and his family—by degrees they excited a diflike in mafter Robert, that in time was fixed into habit, and fell little fhort of averfion.

Young Wenlock's hatred was confirmed by an additional circumftance, he had a growing paffion for the lady Emma, the baron's only daughter, and as love is eagle-eyed, he faw, or fancied he faw her caft an eye of preference on Edmund. An accidental fervice that fhe received from him, had excited her grateful regards and attentions towards him. The inceffant view of his fine perfon and qualities, had perhaps improved her efteem into a ftill fofter fenfation, though fhe was yet ignorant of it, but thought it only the tribute due to gratitude and friendfhip.

One

One Chriſtmas time, the baron and all his family went to viſit a family in Wales—croſſing a ford, the horſe that carried the lady, Emma, who rode behind her couſin Wenlock, ſtumbled and fell down, and threw her off into the water—Edmund diſmounted in a moment, and flew to her aſſiſtance—he took her out ſo quick, that the accident was not known to ſome part of the company—from this time Wenlock ſtrove to undermine Edmund in her eſteem, and ſhe conceived herſelf obliged in juſtice and gratitude to defend him againſt the malicious inſinuatiens of his enemies—ſhe one day aſked Wenlock why he in particular ſhould endeavour to recommend himſelf to her favour, by ſpeaking againſt Edmund, to whom ſhe was under great obligations?—he made but little reply, but the impreſſicn ſunk deep into his rancourous heart—every word in Edmund's behalf was like a poiſoned arrow that rankled in the wound, and grew every day more inflamed—ſometimes he would pretend to extenuate Edmund's ſuppoſed faults, in order to load him with the ſin of ingratitude upon other occaſions—rancour works deepeſt in the heart that ſtrives to conceal it, and when covered by art, frequently puts on the appearance of candour; by theſe means did Wenlock and Markham impoſe upon the credulity of maſter Robert and their other relations, only maſter William ſtood proof againſt all their inſinuatious.——

The ſame autumn that Edmund compleated his eighteenth year, the baron declared his intention of ſending the young men of his houſe to France the following ſpring, to learn

the

the art of war, and fignalize their courage and abilities.

Their ill will towards Edmund was fo well concealed, that his patron had not difcovered it, but it was whifpered among the fervants, who are generally clofe obfervers of the manners of their principals. Edmund was a favorite with them all, which was a ftrong prefumption that he deferved to be fo, for they feldom fhew much regard to dependents, or to fuperiour domeftics, who are generally objects of envy and diflike. Edmund was courteous, but not familiar with them, and by this means gained their affections without foliciting them. Among them was an old ferving man, called Jofeph Howell, this man had formerly ferved the old lord Lovel, and his fon, and when the young lord died, and fir Walter fold the caftle to his brother-in-law, the lord Fitz-Owen, he only of all the old fervants was left in the houfe, to take care of it, and to deliver it into the poffeffion of the new proprietor, who retained him in his fervice—he was a man of few words but much reflection, without troubling himfelf about other peoples affairs, he went filently and properly about his own bufinefs—more folicitous to difcharge his duty, than to recommend himfelf to notice, and not feeming to afpire to any higher office than that of a ferving man. This old man would fix his eyes upon Edmund, whenever he could do it without obfervation—fometimes he would figh deeply, and a tear would ftart from his eye, which he ftrove to conceal from obfervation—one day Edmund furprized him in this tender emotion, as he was wiping his eyes with the

back

back of his hand.—why said he, my good friend, do you look at me so earnestly and affectionately?—because I love you master Edmund, said he, because I wish you well, I thank you kindly, answered Edmund, I am unable to repay your love, otherwise than by returning it, which I do sincerely. I thank you sir, said the old man, that is all I desire, and more than I deserve—do not say so, said Edmund, if I had any better way to thank you, I would not say so much about it, but words are all my inheritance—upon this he shook hands with Joseph, who withdrew hastily to conceal his emotion, saying, God bless you master, and make your fortune equal to your deserts!—I cannot help thinking you were born to a higher station than what you now hold.—you know to the contrary, said Edmund, but Joseph was gone out of sight and hearing.—the notice and observation of strangers, and the affection of individuals, together with that inward consciousness that always attends superior qualities, would sometimes kindle the flames of ambition in Edmund's heart, but he checked them presently by reflecting upon his low birth and dependant station—he was modest yet intrepid, gentle and courteous to all, frank and unreserved to those that loved him, discreet and complaisant to those who hated him, generous and compassionate to the distresses of his fellow creatures in general, humble but not servile to his patron and superiors.—once when he with a manly spirit justified himself against a malicious imputation, his young lord Robert taxed him with pride and arrogance to his kinsmen.

D   Edmund

Edmund denied the charge againſt him with equal ſpirit and modeſty—maſter Robert anſwered him ſharply—how dare you contradict my couſins, do you mean to give them the lye? not in words ſir, ſaid Edmund, but I will behave ſo as that you ſhall not believe them—maſter Robert haughtily bad him be ſilent and know himſelf, and not preſume to contend with men ſo much his ſuperiors in every reſpect—theſe heart-burnings in ſome degree ſubſided by their preparations for going to France. Maſter Robert was to be preſented at court before his departure, and it was expected that he ſhould be knighted. The baron deſigned Edmund to be his eſquire, but this was fruſtrated by his old enemies, who perſuaded Robert to make choice of one of his own domeſtics, called Thomas Hewſon; him did they ſet up as a rival to Edmund, and he took every occaſion to affront him—all that maſter Robert gained by this ſtep, was the contempt of thoſe who ſaw Edmund's merit, and thought it want of diſcernment in him not to diſtinguiſh and reward it—Edmund requeſted of his lord that he might be maſter William's attendant, and when, ſaid he, my patron ſhall be knighted, as I make no doubt he ſhall one day, he has promiſed that I ſhall be his eſquire. —the baron granted Edmund's requeſt, and being freed from ſervitude to the reſt, he was devoted to that of his beloved maſter William, who treated him in public as his principal domeſtic, but in private as his choſen friend and brother.

The whole cabal of his enemies conſulted together in what manner they ſhould vent their

re-

resentment against him, and it was agreed that they should treat him with indifference and neglect, till they should arrive in France, and when there, they should contrive to render his courage suspected, and by putting him upon some desperate enterprize, rid themselves of him for ever. About this time died the great duke of Bedford, to the irreparable loss of the English nation—he was succeeded by Richard Plantagenet, duke of York, as regent of France, of which great part had revolted to Charles the dauphin—frequent actions ensued—cities were lost and won, and continual occasions offered to exercise the courage and abilities of the youth of both nations.

The young men of baron Fitz-Owen's house were recommended particularly to the regent's notice. Master Robert was knighted, with several other young men of family who distinguished themselves by their spirit and activity upon every occasion—the youth were daily employed in warlike exercises and frequent actions, and made their first essay in arms in such a manner as to bring into notice all that deserved it.

Various arts were used by Edmund's enemies to expose him to danger, but all their contrivances recoiled upon themselves, and brought increase of honour upon Edmund's head; he distinguished himself upon so many occasions that sir Robert himself began to pay him more than ordinary regard to the infinite mortification of his kinsmen and relations—they laid many schemes against him, but none took effect.

From this place the characters in the manuscript are effaced by time and moisture—here and there

same

some sentences are legible but not sufficient to persue the thread of the story. Mention is made of several actions in which the young men were engaged——that Edmund distinguished himself by intrepidity in action, by gentleness, humanity and modesty in the cessations—that he attracted the notice of every person of observation, and also that he received personal commendation from the regent.

(The following incidents are clear enough to be transcribed, but the beginning of the next succeeding pages, is obliterated; however we may guess at the beginning by what remains.)

AS foon as the cabal met in fir Robert's tent, mr. Wenlock thus began. You fee my friends that every attempt we make to humble this upftart, turns into applaufe, to raife his pride ftill higher—fomething muft be done, or his praife will go home before us, at our own expence, and we fhall feem only foils to fet off his glories—any thing would I give to the man who fhould execute our vengeance upon him. Stop there coufin Wenlock, faid fir Robert, though I think Edmund proud and vain-glorious, and would join in any fcheme to humble him and make him know himfelf; I will not fuffer any man to ufe fuch bafe methods to effect it. Edmund is brave, and it is beneath an Englifhman to revenge himfelf by unworthy means, if any fuch are ufed I will be the firft man to bring the guilty to juftice, and if I hear another word to this purpofe, I will inform my brother William, who will acquaint Edmund with your mean intentions. Upon this the cabal drew back, and mr. Wenlock protefted that he meant no more than to mortify his pride, and make him know his proper ftation, foon after fir Robert withdrew, and they refumed their deliberations.

Then fpoke Thomas Hewfon, there is a party to be feut out tomorrow night, to intercept a convoy of provifions for the relief of Rouen; I will provoke mr. Edmund to make one of this party, and when he is engaged in the action, I and my companions will draw off, and leave him to the enemy, who I truft will fo handle him, that you fhall no more be troubled with him—this will do, faid mr. Wen-

D 3 lock,

lock, but let it be kept from my two coufins
and only known to ourfelves, if they offer to
be of the party, I will perfuade them off it;
and you Thomas, if you bring this fcheme to
a conclufion, may depend upon my eternal gratitude—and mine, faid Markam, and fo faid
all. The next day the affair was publickly
mentioned, and Hewfon, as he promifed, pro-
voked Edmund to the trial; feveral young
men of family offered themfelves, among the
reft fir Robert and his brother William. Mr.
Wenlock perfuaded them not to go, and fet
the danger of the enterprize in the ftrongeft
colours—at laft fir Robert complained of the
tooth-ach, and was confined to his tent, Edmund waited on him, and judging by the ardor of his own courage of that of his patron,
thus befpoke him. I am greatly concerned
dear fir, that we cannot have your company
at night, but as I know what you will fuffer in
being abfent, I would beg the favour of you to
let me ufe your arms and device, and I will
promife not to difgrace them. No Edmund
I cannot confent to that, I thank you for your
noble offer, and will remember it to your advantage, but I cannot wear honours of another
man's getting; you have awakened me to a
fenfe of my duty, I will go with you, and
contend with you for glory, and William fhall
do the fame.

In a few hours they were ready to fet out;
Wenlock and Markham, and their dependants
found themfelves engaged in honour to go
upon an enterprize they never intended, and
fet out with heavy hearts to join the party.—
they marched in filence in the horrors of a dark
night,

night, and wet roads; they met the convoy where they expected, and a sharp engagement ensued. The victory was some time doubtful, but the moon rising on the backs of the English, gave them the advantage. They saw the disposition of their enemies, and availed themselves of it—Edmund advanced the foremost of the party, he drew out the leader on the French side, he slew him. Mr. William pressed forward to assist his friend, sir Robert to defend his brother—Wenlock and Markham from shame to stay behind.

Thomas Hewson and his associates drew back on their side, the French perceived it and persued the advantage. Edmund pushed them in front, the young nobles all followed him; they broke through the detachment, and stopped the waggons. The officer who commanded the party, encouraged them to go on; the defeat was soon compleat, and the provisions carried in triumph to the English camp.

Edmund was presented to the regent as the man to whom the victory was chiefly owing—not a tongue presumed to lift itself against him, even malice and envy were silenced.

Approach young man, said the regent, that I may confer upon you the honour of knighthood, which you have well deserved.——Mr. Wenlock could no longer forbear speaking, knighthood, said he, is an order belonging to gentlemen, it cannot be conferred on a peasant—what say you sir, said the regent, is this youth a peasant? he is, said Wenlock. let him deny it if he can. Edmund with a modest bow; it is true indeed I am a peasant, and

this

this honour is too great for me, I have only done my duty. The duke of York whose pride of birth equalled any man living or dead, sheathed his sword immediately. Though said he, I cannot reward you as I intended, I will take care that you shall have a large share in the spoils of this night, and I declare publickly that you stand first in the list of gallant men in this engagement.

Thomas Hewson and his associates made a poor figure in their return ; they were publickly reproved for their backwardness. Hewson was wounded in body, and more in mind, for the ill success of his ill laid design. He could not hold up his head before Edmund, who unconscious of their malice administered every kind of comfort to them. He spoke in their behalf to the commanding officer, imputing their conduct to unavoidable accidents. He visited them privately, he gave them a part of the spoils allotted to himself, by every act of valour and courtesy, he strove to engage those hearts that hated, envied and maligned him, but where hatred arises from envy of superior qualities. every display of those qualities increases the cause from whence it arises.

Another pause ensues.

The young nobles and gentlemen who distinguished Edmund, were prevented from raising him to preferment by the insinuations of Wenlock and his associates, he never failed to set before them his low descent, his pride and arrogance in presuming to rank with gentlemen.

Here

Here the manuscript is not legible for a long way. There is mention about this time of the death of the lady Fitz-Owen, but not the cause. Wenlock rejoiced to find that his schemes took effect that they should be recalled at the approach of winter. The baron was glad of a pretence to send for them home, for he could no longer endure the absence of his children after the loss of their mother.

The manuscript again defaced by moisture for many leaves, at length the letters come more legible, and the remainder of it is quite perfect every page.

FROM

FROM the time the young men returned from France, the enemies of Edmund employed their utmoſt abilities to ruin him in the baron's opinion, and get him diſmiſſed from the family—they inſinuated a thouſand things againſt him that happened, as they ſaid, during his reſidence in France, and therefore could not be known to his maſter; but when the baron privately enquired' of his two elder ſons, he found there was no truth in their reports. Sir Robert though he did not love him, ſcorned to join in untruths againſt him. Mr. William ſpoke of him with the warmth of fraternal affection—the baron perceived that his kinſmen diſliked Edmund, but his own good heart hindered him from ſeeing the baſeneſs of theirs —it is ſaid that continual dropping will wear away a ſtone, ſo did their inceſſant reports by inſenſible degrees produce a coolneſs in his patron's behaviour towards him—if he behaved with manly ſpirit, is was miſconſtrued into pride and arrogance, his generoſity was imprudence, his humility was hippocriſy, the better to cover his ambition—Edmund bore patiently all the indignities that were thrown upon him, and though he felt them ſeverely in his boſom, yet he ſcorned to juſtify his conduct at the expence of of even his enemies—perhaps his gentle ſpirit might at length have ſunk under this treatment, but providence interpoſed in his behalf, and by accidental circumſtances, conducted him imperceptibly towards the criſis of his fate.

Father Oſwald who had been preceptor to the young men, had a ſtrong affection for Edmund,

mund, from a thorough knowledge of his heart—he faw through the mean aftifices that were uſed to undermine him in his patron's favour, he watched their machinations and ſtrove to fruſtrate their deſigns.

This good man uſed frequently to walk out with Edmund, they converſed upon various ſubjects, and the youth would lament to him the unhappineſs of his ſituation, and the peculiar circumſtances that attended him—the father by his wholeſome advice comforted his drooping heart, and cenfirmed his patience and fortitude to bear unavoidable evils, by conſcious innocence, and the aſſurance of a future and eternal reward.

One day as they were walking in a wood near the caſtle, Edmund aſked the father what meant the preparations for building, the cutting down trees and burning of bricks.—what faid Oſwald, have not you heard that my lord is going to build a new apartment on the weſt fide of the caſtle, and why faid Edmund, ſhould my lord be at that expence when there is one on the eaſt fide that is never occupied?—that apartment, faid the friar, you muſt have obſerved is always ſhut up; I have obſerved it often, faid Edmund, but I never preſumed to aſk any queſtions about it—you had then, faid Oſwald, leſs curioſity and more diſcretion than is common at your age. You have raiſed my curioſity, faid Edmund, and if it be not improper I beg you to gratify it—we are alone, faid Oſwald, and I am ſo well aſſured of your prudence, that I will explain this myſtery in ſome degree to you.

You

You muſt know that apartment was occupied by the laſt lord Lovel when he was a batchelor—he married in his father's life time, who gave up his own apartment to him, and offered to retire to this himſelf, but the ſon would not permit him, he choſe to ſleep here, rather than in any other ; he had been married about three months when his father the old lord died of a fever ; about twelve months after his marriage, he was called upon to attend the king, Henry the fouth, on an expedition into Wales, whither he was attended by many of his dependants—he left his lady big with child, and full of care and anxiety for his ſafety and return.

After the king had chaſtiſed the rebels, and obtained the victory, the lord Lovel was expected home every day—various reports were ſent home before him, one meſſenger brought an account of his health and ſafety—ſoon after another came with bad news, that he was ſlain in battle—his kinſman, ſir Walter Lovel came here on a viſit to comfort the lady, and he waited to receive his kinſman at his return.— it was he that brought the news of the ſad event of the battle to the lady Lovel.

She fainted away at the relation, but when ſhe revived, exerted the utmoſt reſolution, ſaying it was her duty to bear this dreadful ſtroke with chriſtian fortitude and patience, eſpecially in regard to the child ſhe went with, the laſt remains of her beloved huſband, and the undoubted heir of a noble houſe. For ſeveral days ſhe ſeemed an example of patience and reſignation, but then all at once ſhe renounced them, and broke out into paſſionate and frantic
                                        excla-

exclamations, fhe faid that her dear lord was bafely murdered, that his ghoft had appeared to her and revealed his fate—fhe called upon heaven and earth to revenge her wrongs, faying fhe would never ceafe complaining to God and the king for vengeance and juftice.

Upon this fir Walter told the fervants that lady Lovel was diftracted, from grief for the death of her lord, that his regard for her was as ftrong as ever, and that if fhe recovered he would himfelf be her comforter and marry her. In the mean time fhe was confined in this very apartment and in lefs than a month the poor lady died.—fhe lies buried in the family vault in it. Auftin's church in the village. Sir Walter took poffeffion of the caftle and all the other eftates, and affumed the title of lord Lovel.

Soon after it was reported that the caftle was haunted, and that the ghofts of lord and lady Lovel had been feen by feveral of the fervants.—whoever went into this apartment were terrified by uncommon noifes and ftrange appearances; at length this apartment was wholly fhut up, and the fervants were forbid to enter it, or to talk of any thing relating to it; however the ftory did not ftop here, it was whifpered about that the new lord Lovel was fo difturbed every night that he could not fleep in quiet, and being at laft tired of the place, he fold the caftle and eftate of his anceftors, to his brother-in-law the lord Fitz-Owen who now enjoys it, and left this country.

All this is news to me, faid Edmund, but father, tell me what grounds there were for the lady's fufpicion that her lord died unfairly. —alas! faid Ofwald, that is only known to

E God.

God.—there was ftrange thoughts in the minds of many at that time, I had mine, but I will not difclofe them, not even to you.—I will not injure thofe who may be innocent, and I leave it to providence, who will doubtlefs in its own beft time and manner punifh the guilty.—but let what I have told you be as if you had never heard it.

I thank you for thefe marks of your efteem and confidence, faid Edmund, be affured that I will not abufe it, nor do I defire to pry into fecrets not proper to be revealed, I entirely approve your difcretion, and acquiefe in your conclufion, that providence will in its own time vindicate its ways to man ; if it were not for that truft my fituation would be infupportable. I ftrive earneftly to deferve the efteem and favour of good men, I endeavour to regulate my conduct fo as to avoid giving offence to any man, but I fee with infinite pain that it is impoffible for me to gain thefe points. I fee it too with great concern, faid Ofwald, and every thing that I can fay and do in your favour is mifconftrued, and by feeking to do you fervice, I lofe my own influence, but I will never give my fanction to acts of injuftice, nor join to opprefs innocence. My dear child put your truft in God, he who brought light out of darknefs, can bring good out of evil.— I hope and truft fo, faid Edmund, but father, if my enemies fhould prevail againft me, if my lord fhould believe their ftories againft me, and I fhould be put out of the houfe with difgrace what will become of me ? I have nothing but my character to depend upon, if I lofe that I lofe every thing, and I fee they feek no lefs
than

than my ruin. Truft in my lord's honour and juftice, replied Ofwald, he knows your virtue, and he is not ignorant of their ill will towards you. I know my lord's juftice too well to doubt, faid Edmund, but would it not be better to rid him of this trouble, and his family of an incumbrance, I would gladly do fomething for myfelf, but cannot without my lord's recommendation, and fuch is my fituation, that I fear to afk for a difmiffion would be accounted bafe ingratitude; befide when I think of leaving this houfe, my heart relucts againft it, and tells me I cannot be happy out of it; yet I think I could return to a peafant's life with chearfulnefs, rather than live in a palace under difdain and contempt. Have patience a little longer, my fon, faid Ofwald, I will think of fome way to ferve you, and to reprefent your grievances to my lord, without offence to either; perhaps the caufes may be removed, continue to obferve the fame irreproachable conduct, and be affured that heaven will defend your innocence and defeat the unjuft defigns of your enemies; let us now return home.

About a week after this conference, Edmund had walked out in the fields ruminating on the difagreeable circumftances of his fituation. Infenfible of the time he had been out feveral hours without perceiving how the day wore away, when he heard himfelf called by name feveral times; looking backward he faw his friend mr. William, and hallowed to him. He came running towards him, and leaping over the ftyle, ftood ftill a while to recover his breath. What is the matter, fir, faid Edmund, your looks befpeaks fome tidings of importance:

tance : with a look of tender concern and affection, the youth preffed his hand and fpoke.
My dear Edmund, you muft come home with
me directly, your old enemies have united
to ruin you with my father, my brother
Robert has declared that he thinks there will
be no peace in our family till you are difmiffed
from it, and told my father, he hoped he
would not break with his kinfmen rather than
give up Edmund. But what do they lay to my
charge ? faid Edmund. I cannot rightly underftand, anfwered William, for they make a
great myftery of it, fomething of great confequence they fay, but they will not tell me what,
however, my father has told them that they
muft bring their accufation before your face,
and he will have you anfwer them publickly ; I
have been feeking you this hour to inform you
of this, that you might, be prepared to defend
yourfelf againft your accufers. God reward
you fir, faid Edmund, for all your goodnefs to
me ? I fee they are determined to ruin me if
poffible ; I fhall be compelled to leave the caftle, but whatever becomes of me, be affured
you fhall have no caufe to blufh for your kindnefs and partiality to your Edmund. I know
it, I am fure of it, faid William, and here I
fwear to you as Jonathan did to David, I befeech heaven to blefs me, as my friendfhip to
you fhall be fteady and inviolable !—only fo
long as I fhall deferve fo great a bleffing, interrupted Edmund.—I know your worth and
honour, continued William, and fuch is my
confidence in your merit, that I firmly believe
heaven defigns you for fomething extraordinary, and I expect that fome great and unfore-
feen

seen event will raise you to the rank and station to which you appear to belong; promise me therefore, that whatever may be your fate you will preserve the same friendship for me that I bear to you. Edmund was so much affected that he could not answer but in broken sentences. Oh my friend, my master, I vow, I promise, my heart promises!—he kneeled down with clapped hands and uplifted eyes. William kneeled by him, and they invoked the supreme to witness to their friendship and implored his blessing upon it; they then rose up and embraced each other, while tears of cordial affection bedewed their cheeks.

As soon as they were able to speak, Edmund conjured his friend not to expose himself to the displeasure of his family out of kindness to him. I submit to the will of heaven, said he, I wait with patience its disposal of me, if I leave the castle I will find means to inform you of my fate and fortunes. I hope, said William, that things may yet be accommodated, but do not take any resolution, let us act as occasions arise.

In this manner these amiable youths conferred, till they arrived at the castle. The baron was sitting in the great hall on a high chair with a footstep before, with the state and dignity of a judge, before him stood father Oswald, as pleading the cause for himself and Edmund. Round the baron's chair stood his eldest son and his kinsmen, with their principal domestics. The old servant, Joseph, at some distance, with his head leaning forward as listening with the utmost attention to what passed. Mr. William approached the chair.—my lord,

E 3   I have

I have found Edmund, and brought him to answer for himself.—you have done well, said the
baron.—Edmund come hither, you are charged
with some indiscretions, for I cannot properly
call them crimes, I am resolved to do justice
between you and your accusers, I shall therefore hear you as well as them, for no man
ought to be condemned unheard. My lord,
said Edmund, with equal modesty and intrepidity, I demand my trial, if I shall be found
guilty of any crimes against my benefactor,
let me be punished with the utmost rigor.—
but if as I trust no such charge can be proved
against me, I know your goodness too well to
doubt that you will do justice to me, as well
as to others, and if it should so happen that
by the misrepresentations of my enemies (who
have long sought my ruin privately, and now
avow it publickly) if by their artifices your
lordship should be induced to think me guilty,
I would submit to your sentence in silence,
and appeal to another tribunal. See, said mr.
Wenlock, the confidence of the fellow! he
already supposes that my lord must be in the
wrong if he condemns him, and then this
meek creature will appeal to another tribunal,
to whose will he appeal, I desire he may be
made to explain himself?—that I will immediately, said Edmund, without being compelled,
I only meant to appeal to heaven that best
knows my innocence. 'Tis true, said the
baron, and no offence to any one; man can
only judge by appearances, but heaven knows
the heart; let every one of you bear this in
mind, that you may not bring a false accusation, nor justify yourselves by concealing the
truth.

truth. Edmund, I am informed that Ofwald and you have made very free with me and my family, in fome of your converfations; you were heard to cenfure me for the abfurdity of building a new apartment on the weft fide of the caftle when there was one on the eaft fide uninhabited, Ofwald faid, that apartment was fhut up becaufe it was haunted, that fome fhocking murther had been committed there, adding many particulars concerning lord Lovel's family, fuch as he could not know the truth of, and if he had known, was imprudent to reveal ; but further you complained of illtreatment here, and mentioned an intention to leave the caftle and feek your fortune elfewhere. I fhall examine into all thefe particulars in turn, at prefent I defire you Edmund, to relate all that you can remember of the converfation that paffed between you and Ofwald in the wood laft Monday. Good God, faid Edmund ? is it poffible that any perfon could put fuch a conftruction upon fo innocent a converfation ?

Tell me then, faid the baron the particulars of it ? I will my lord as nearly as my memory will allow me.—accordingly he related moft of the converfation that paffed in the wood, but in the part that concerned the family of Lovel he abbreviated as much as poffible. Ofwald's countenance cleared up, for he had done the fame before Edmund came. The baron called to his eldeft fon, you hear, fir Robert, what both parties fay, I have heard them feparately, neither of them knew what the other would fay, yet their accounts agree almoft to a word. I confefs they do fo, anfwered fir Robert, but fir it is very bold and

pre-

presuming for them to speak of our family affairs in such a manner, if my uncle lord Lovel
should come to know it, he would punish them
severely, and if his honour is reflected upon,
it becomes us to resent and to punish it. Here
mr. Wenlock broke out into passion and offered
to swear to the truth of his accusation. Be
silent Dick, said the baron, I shall judge for
myself. I protest, said he to sir Robert, I never heard so much as Oswald has now told me
concerning the deaths of lord and lady Lovel,
I think it is best to let such stories alone till
they die away of themselves. I had indeed
heard of an idle story of the east apartments
being haunted when first I came hither, and
my brother advised me to shut it up till it should
be forgotten; but what has now been said,
has suggested a thought that may make that
apartment useful in future. I have thought
of a punishment for Edmund that will stop
the mouth of his accusers for the present, and
as I hope to establish his credit with every body. Edmund will you undertake this adventure for me ?—what adventure my lord, said
Edmund ?—there is nothing I would not undertake to show my gratitude and fidelity to
you; as to my courage, I would show that at
the expence of my malicious accusers, if respect to my lord's blood did not tie up my
hands; as I am situated I beg it may be put
to the proof in that way that is most for my
master's service. That is well said, cried the
baron, as to your enemies, I am thinking how
to separate you from them effectually, of that
I shall speak hereafter.—I am going to try
Edmund's courage, he shall sleep three nights
in

in the eaſt apartment, and that he may teſtiſy
to all whether it be haunted or not ; afterwards
I will have that apartment ſet in order, and
my eldeſt ſon ſhall take it for his own, it will
ſpare me ſome expence and anſwer my purpoſe as well or better, will you conſent Edmund ?—with all heart my lord, ſaid Edmund,
I have not wilfully offended God or man, I
have therefore nothing to ſear.—brave boy !
ſaid my lord, I am not deceived in you, nor
ſhall you be deceived in your reliance on me,
you ſhall ſleep in that apartment to night, and
to morrow I will have ſome private talk with
you.—do you Oſwald go with me, I want to
have ſome converſation with you.—the reſt of.
you retire to your ſtudies and buſineſs, I will
meet you at dinner.

Edmund retired to his own chamber, and
Oſwald was ſhut up with the baron ; he de-
ſended Edmund's cauſe and his own, and laid
open as much as he knew of the malice and
deſigns of his enemies.—the baron expreſſed
much concern at the untimely deaths of lord
and lady Lovel, and deſired Oſwald to be circum-
ſpect in regard to what he had to ſay of the circumſtances of them ; adding that he was both
innocent and ignorant of any treachery towards
either of them. Oſwald excuſed himſelf for
his communications to Edmund, ſaying, they
ſell undeſignedly into the ſubject, and that he
mentioned it in confidence to him only.

The baron ſent orders to the young men to
come to dinner, but they reſuſed to meet Edmund at table, according he ate in the ſteward's
apartment.—after dinner the baron tried to reconcile his kinſmen to Edmund, but ſound it
im-

impoffible.—they found their defigns laid open, and judging of him by themfelves, thought it impoffible to forgive or be forgiven.—he ordered them to keep in feparate apartments, he took his eldeft fon for his own companion, as being the moft reafonable of the malecontents ; he ordered his kinfmen to keep their own apartment, with a fervant to watch their motions. Mr. William had Ofwald for his companion, he ordered old Jofeph to attend on Edmund, to ferve him at fupper, and at the hour of nine to conduct him to the haunted apartment. Edmund defired that he might have a light and his fword, left his enemies fhould endeavour to furprife him.—the baron thought his requeft reafonable, and complied with it.

There was a great fearch to find the key of the apartment at laft it was difcovered by Edmund himfelf among a parcel of old rufty keys in a lumber room. The baron fent the young men their fuppers to their refpective apartments.—Edmund declined eating, and defired to be conducted to his apartment.—he was accompanied by moft of the fervants to the door of it, they wifhed him fuccefs, and prayed for him as if he had been going to execution.

The door was with great difficulty unlocked, and Jofeph gave Edmund a lighted lamp and wifhed him a good night ; he returned his good wifhes to them all with the utmoft chearfulnefs, took the key on the infide the door and difmiffed them.

He then took a furvey of his chamber, the furniture by long neglect was decayed and dropping to pieces ; the bed was devoured by
the

the moths, and occupied by the rats, who had built their nests there with impunity for many generations. The bedding was very damp, for the rain had forced its way through the ceiling, he determined therefore to lie down in his clothes. There were two doors on the further side of the room with keys in them; being not at all sleepy, he resolved to examine them, he attempted one lock and opened it with ease, he went into a large dining room, the furniture of which was in the same tattered condition; out of this was a large closet with some books in it, and hung round with coats of arms with genealogies and alliances of the house of Lovel; he amused himself here some minutes and then returned into the bed chamber.

He recollected the other door, and resolved to see where it led to; the key was rusted into the lock, and resisted his attempts, he set the lamp on the ground, and exerting all his strength opened the door, and at the same instant the wind of it blew out the lamp, and left him in utter darkness.—at the same moment he heard a hollow rustling noise like that of a person coming through a narrow passage. Till this moment not one idea of fear had come near the mind of Edmund, but just then all the concurrent circumstances of his situation struck upon his heart, and gave him a new and disagreeable sensation.—he paused a while and recollecting himself, cried out aloud, what should I fear, I have not wilfully offended God or man, why then should I doubt protection: but I have not yet implored the divine assistance, how then can I expect it.—upon this he
kneeled

kneeled down and prayed earneftly, refigning himfelf wholy to the will of heaven ; while he was yet fpeaking his courage returned, and he refumed his ufual confidence ; again he approached the door from whence the noife proceeded, he thought he faw a glimmering light upon a ftaircafe before him.—if, faid he, this apartment is haunted I will ufe my endeavours to difcover the caufe of it, and if the fpirit appears vifibly, I will fpeak to it.

He was preparing to defcend the ftaircafe, when he heard feveral knocks at the door by which he firft entered the room, and ftepping backward the door was clapped too with great violence. Again fear attacked him, but he refifted it, and boldly cried out, who is there?—a voice at the outer door anfwered, 'tis I—Jofeph, your friend !—what do you want, faid Edmund ?—I have brought you fome wood to make a fire, faid Jofeph.—I thank you kindly, faid Edmund, but my lamp is gone out, I will try to find the door however.—after fome trouble he found and opened it, and was not forry to fee his friend Jofeph with a light in one hand and a flaggon of beer in the other, and a faggot upon his fhoulder—I come, faid the good old man to bring you fomething to keep up your fpirits, the evening is cold, I know this room wants airing, and befide that my mafter, I think your prefent undertaking requires a little affiftance.

My good friend, faid Edmund, I never fhall be able to deferve or requite your kindnefs to me.—my dear fir, you always deferved more than I could do for you, and I think I fhall yet live to fee you defeat the defigns of your enemies,

.enemies, and acknowledge the services.of your
friends.—alas, said Edmund, I see little pros-
pect of that!—I see, said Joseph, something
that persuades me you are designed for great
things, and I perceive that things are working
about to some great end; have courage my
.master, my heart beats strangely high upon
.your account!—you make me smile, said Edmund,—I am glad to see it sir, may you smile
all the rest of your life.—I thank your honest
affection, returned. Edmund, though it is too
partial to me,—you had better go to bed however, if it is known that you visit me here, it
will be bad for us both.—so I will presently,
but please God I will come here again to morrow night when all the family are a bed, and
I will tell you some things that you never yet
.heard.—but pray tell me, said Edmund, where
does that door lead to? —upon a passage that
ends in a staircase that leads to the lower rooms,
.and there is likewise a door out of that passage
into the dining room —and what rooms are
there below stairs, said Edmund? the same as
above, replied he,—very well, then I wish you
a good night, we will talk further to morrow.
—aye to morrow night, and in this place my
dear master.—why do you call me your master, I never was nor ever can be your master?
—God only knows that, said the good old
man, good night, and heaven bless you!——
good night my worthy friend!

Joseph withdrew, and Edmund returned to
the other door and attempted several times to
open it in vain, his hands were benumbed and
tired, at length he gave over, he made a fire
in the chimney, placed the lamp on a table,

F   opened

opened one of the window shutters to admit the day-light; he then recommended himself to the divine protection, and threw himself upon the bed, he presently fell asleep, till the sun saluted him with his orient beams through the window he had opened.

As soon as he was perfectly awake he strove to recollect his dreams; he thought that he heard people coming up the staircase that he had a glimpse of; that the door opened, and there entered a warrior, leading a lady by the hand, who was young and beautiful, but pale and wan; the man was dressed in complete armour, and his helmet down; they approached the bed; they undrew the curtains; he thought the man said, is this our child? the woman replied it is, and the hour approaches that he shall be known for such; they then separated, and one stood on each side of the bed. their hands met over his head, and they gave him a solemn benediction.—he strove to rise and pay them his respects, but they forbid him, and the lady said, sleep in peace, oh Edmund! for those who are the true possessors of this apartment are employed in thy preservation; sleep on sweet hope of a house that is thought past hope! upon this he thought they withdrew and went out at the same door by which they entered, and he heard them descend the stairs.—after this he thought he followed a funeral as chief mourner, he saw the whole procession and heard the ceremonies performed; he was snatched away from this mournful scene to one of a contrary kind, a stately feast, at which he presided, and he heard himself congratulated as a husband and

a faa father; his friend William fat by his fide, and his happinefs was complete.—every fucceeding idea was happinefs without allay, and his mind was not idle a moment till the morning fun awakened him; he perfectly remembered his dreams, and meditated what all thefe things fhould portend; am I then, faid he, not Edmund Tywford, but fomebody of confequence in whofe fate fo many people are interefted. Vain thought, that muft have arifen from the partial fuggeftion of my two friends, mr. William and old Jofeph!

. He lay reflecting upon his dreams, when a fervant knocked at his door, and told him it was paft fix o'clock, and the baron expected him to breakfaft in an hour; he rofe immediately, paid his tribute of thanks to heaven for its protection, and went from his chamber in high health and fpirits.

He walked in the garden till the hour of breakfaft, and then attended the baron. Good morrow, Edmund! faid he, how have you refted in your new apartment? extremely well my lord, anfwered he. I am glad to hear it, faid the baron, but I did not know your accommodations were fo bad, as Jofeph tells me they are. —'tis of no confequence, faid Edmund, if they were much worfe I could difpenfe with them for three nights.—very well, faid the baron, you are a brave lad, I am fatisfied with you, and will excufe the other two nights.—but my lord I will not be excufed, no one fhall have reafon to fufpect my courage, I am determined to go through the remaining nights upon many accounts.—that fhall be as you pleafe, faid my lord.—I think of you as you deferve,

fo

so well that I shall ask your advice by and by
in some affairs of consequence.—my life and
services are yours my lord, command them
freely.—let Ofwald be called in, said my lord,
he shall be one of our consultation.—he came.
—the servants were dismissed, and the baron
spoke as follows. Edmund, when first I took
you into my family it was at the request of
my sons and kinsmen, I bear witness to your
good behaviour, you have not deserved to lose
their esteem, but nevertheless I have observed
for some years past, that all but my son William have set their faces against you; I see
their meanness and I perceive their motives,
but they are and must be my relations, and I
would rather govern them by love than fear.
I love and esteem your virtues, I cannot give
you up to gratify their humours; my son William has lost the affections of the rest, for
that he bears to you; but he has increased
my regard for him; I think myself bound in
honour to him and you, to provide for you;
I cannot do it as I wished under my own
roof, if you stay here I see nothing but confusion in my family, yet I cannot put you out
of it disgracefully; I want to think of some
way to prefer you, that you may leave this
house with honour, and I desire both of you
to give me your advice in this matter. If
Edmund will tell me what way I can employ
him to his own honour and my advantage, I
am ready to do it, let him propose, it and
Ofwald shall moderate between us.

Here he stopped, and Edmund whose sighs
almost choaked him, threw himself at the
baron's feet, and wet his hand with his tears.

oh,

oh, my noble generous benefactor!—do you condefcend to confult fuch a one as me upon the ftate of your family? does your moft amiable and beloved fon incur the ill will of his brothers and kinfmen for my fake? what am I that I fhould difturb the peace of this noble family? oh my lord, fend me away directly! I fhould be unworthy to live if I did not earneftly endeavour to reftore your happinefs; you have given me a noble education, and I truft I fhall not difgrace it; if you will recommend me and give me a character, I fear not to make my own fortune. The baron wiped his eyes, I wifh to do this my child, but in what way?—my lord, faid Edmund, I will open my heart, I have ferved with credit in the army, and I fhould prefer a foldier's life. You pleafe me well, faid the baron, I will ferd you to France, and give you a recommendation to the regent, he knows you perfonally, and will prefer you for my fake and for your own merit.—my lord you overwhelm me with your goodnefs; I am but your creature and my life fhall be devoted to your fervice.—but faid the baron, how to difpofe of you till the fpring?—that faid Ofwald may be thought of at leifure, I am glad that you have refolved, and I congratulate you both,—the baron put an end to the converfation by defiring Edmund to go with him into the manage to fee his horfes.—he ordered Ofwald to acquaint his fon William with all that had paffed, and to try to perfuade the young men to meet Edmund and William at dinner.

The baron took Edmund with him into his manage to fee fome horfes he had lately purchafed,

chafed, while they were examining the beauties and defects of thefe noble and ufeful ani-
mals: Edmund declared that he preferred Ca-
radoc, a horfe he had broke himfelf, to any
other in my lord's ftables.—then faid the baron, I will give him to you, you fhall go upon
him to feek your fortune.—he made new acknowledgements for this gift, and declared he
would prize it highly for the giver's fake.——
but I fhall not part with you yet, faid my lord,
I will firft carry all my points with thefe faucy
boys, and oblige them to do you juftice.——
you have already done that, faid Edmund, and
I will not fuffer any of your lordfhip's blood
to undergo any further humiliation upon my
account.—I think, with humble fubmiffion to
your better judgment, the fooner I go hence
the better.

While they were fpeaking, Ofwald came to
them, and faid that the young men had abfo-
lutely refufed to dine at the table if Edmund
was prefent.—'tis well, faid the baron, I fhall
find a way to punifh their contumacy hereafter,
I will make them know that I am the mafter
here.—Edmund and you Ofwald, fhall fpend
the day in my apartment above ftairs.—William fhall dine with me alone, and I will acquaint him with our determination; my fon
Robert and his cabal fhall be prifoners in the
great parlour; Edmund fhall according to his
own defire fpend this and the following night
in the haunted apartment, and this for his
fake and my own, for if I fhould now contradict my former orders, it would fubject us both
to their impertinent reflections.

He

He then took Ofwald afide, and charged him not to let Edmund go out of his fight, for it he fhould come in the way of thofe implacable enemies, he trembled for the confequences.—he then walked.back to the ftables, and the two friends returned into the houfe.

They had a long converfation on various fubjects, in the courfe of it Edmund acquainted Ofwald with all that had paffed between him and Jofeph the preceeding night, the curiofity he had raifed in him, and his promife to gratify it the night following. I wifh, faid Ofwald, you would permit me to be one of your party? how can that be, faid Edmund?—— we fhall be watched perhaps, and if difcovered, what excufe can you make for coming there? befide if it were known I fhall be branded with the imputation of cowardice, and though I have borne much, I will not promife to bear that patiently.—never fear it, replied Ofwald, I will fpeak to Jofeph about it, and after prayers are over and the family gone to bed, I will fteal away from my own chamber and come to you, I am ftrongly interefted in your affairs, and I cannot be eafy unlefs you will receive me into your company, I will bind myfelf to fecrecy in any manner you fhall enjoin,—your word is fufficient, faid Edmund, I have as much reafon to truft you, father, as any man living, I fhould be ungrateful to refufe you any thing in my power to grant; but fuppofe the apartment fhould really be haunted, would you have refolution enough to perfue the adventure to a difcovery?—I hope fo, faid Ofwald, but have you any reafon to believe it is?—I have, faid Edmund, but I have

not

not opened my lips upon this fubject to any
creature but yourfelf; this night I purpofe, if
heaven permit, to go all over the rooms, and
though I had formed this defign, I will confels
that your company will ftrengthen my refolution, I will have no referves to you in any refpect, but I muft put a feal upon your lips.
Ofwald fwore fecrecy till he fhould be permitted to difclose the myfteries of that apartment, and both of them waited in folemn expectation the event of the approaching night.

In the afternoon mr. William was allowed
to vifit his friend, an affecting interview paffed
between them, he lamented the neceffity of
Edmund's departure, and they took a folemn
leave of each other, as if they foreboded it
would be long e'er they fhould meet again.

About the fame hour as the preceeding evening, Jofeph came to conduct Edmund to his
apartment.   You will find better accommodations than you had laft night, faid he, and all
by my lord's own order.   I every hour receive
fome new proof of his goodnefs, faid Edmund.
When they arrived he found a good fire in the
chamber, and a table covered with cold meats
and a flaggon of ftrong beer.—fit down and
get your fupper my dear mafter, faid Jofeph,
I muft attend my lord, but as foon as the family are gone to bed I will vifit you again.—
do fo, faid Edmund, but firft fee father Ofwald, he has fomething to fay to you, you
may truft him, for I have no fecrets from him.
—well fir I will fee him if you defire it, and I
will come to you as foon as poffible.—fo faying he went his way and Edmund fat down to
fupper.

After

After a moderate refreshment he kneeled down and prayed with the greatest fervency, he refigned himself to the difpofal of heaven; I am nothing, faid he, I defire to be nothing but what thou, O Lord, pleafeft to make me, if it is thy will that I fhould return to my former obfcurity, be it obeyed with chearfulnefs! and if thou art pleafed to exalt me, I will look up to thee as the only fountain of honour and dignity. While he prayed he felt an enlargement of heart beyond what he had ever experienced before; all idle fears were difperfed, and his heart glowed with divine love and affiance; he feemed raifed above the world and all its perfuits; he continued wrapt up in mental devotion, till a knocking at the door obliged him to rife and let in his two friends, who came without fhoes and on tiptoe to vifit him.

Save you my fon, faid the friar, you look chearful and happy!—I am fo father, faid Edmund, I have refigned myfelf to the difpofal of heaven, and I find my heart ftrengthened above what I can exprefs.—heaven be praifed! faid Ofwald, I believe you are defigned for great things my fon.—what, do you too encourage my ambition? fays Edmund, ftrange concurrence of circumftances! fit down my friends, and do you my good Jofeph, tell me the particulars you promifed laft night, they drew their chairs round the fire and Jofeph began as follows.

You have heard of the untimely death of the late lord Lovel, my noble and worthy mafter, perhaps you may alfo have heard that from that time this apartment was haunted; what paffed the other day, when my lord
queftioned

queftioned you both on this head, brought all
the circumftances frefh into my mind; you
faid there were fufpicions that he came not
fairly to his end, I truft you both and will
fpeak what I know of it; there was a perfon
fufpected of this murther, and whom do you
think it was?—you muft fpeak out, faid Ofwald.—why then faid Jofeph, it was the prefent lord Lovel.—you fpeak my thoughts, faid
Ofwald, but proceed to the proofs? I will,
faid Jofeph, from the time that my lord's
death was reported, there was ftrange whif-
perings and confultations between the new
lord and fome of the fervants; there was a
deal of private bufinefs carried on in this apartment; foon after they gave out that my poor
lady was diftracted, but fhe threw out ftrong
expreffions that favoured nothing of madnefs;
fhe faid that the ghoft of her departed lord
had appeared to her, and revealed the circumftances of this murther.—none of the fervants
but one were permitted to fee her. At this
very time fir Walter, the new lord, had the
cruelty to offer love to her, he urged her to
marry him, and one of her women overheard
her fay, fhe would fooner die than give her
hand to the man who caufed the death of her
lord; foon after this we were told my lady
was dead. The lord Lovel made a publick
and fumptuous funeral for her.—that is true,
faid Ofwald, for I was a novice and affifted at
it.

Well, fays Jofeph, now comes my part of
the ftory. As I was coming home from the
buriall overtook Roger our plowman.—faid he,
what think you of this burying?—what fhould
I think,

I think, faid I, but that we have loft the beft mafter and lady that we fhall ever know?—God he knows, quoth Roger, whether they be living or dead, but if ever I faw my lady in my life, I faw her alive the night they fay fhe died.—I tried to convince him that he was miftaken, but he offered to take his oath, that the very night they faid fhe died, he faw her come out at the garden gate into the fields, that fhe often ftopped like a perfon in pain, and then went forward again until he loft fight of her.—now it is certain that her time was out, and fhe expected to lay down every day, and they did not pretend that fhe died in childbed. I thought upon what I heard, but nothing I faid.—Roger told the fame ftory to another fervant; fo he was called to an account, the ftory was hufhed up, and the foolifh fellow faid, he was verily perfuaded it was her ghoft that he faw. Now you muft take notice that from this time, they began to talk about that this apartment was troubled, and not only this, but at laft the new lord could not fleep in quiet in his own room, and this induced him to fell the caftle to his brother-in-law, and get out of this country as faft as poffible.—he took moft of the fervants away with him, and Roger among the reft.—as for me, they thought I knew nothing, and fo they left me behind. but I was neither blind nor deaf, though I could hear and fee, and fay nothing.

This is a dark ftory, faid Ofwald, it is fo faid Edmund, but why fhould Jofeph feem to think it concerns me in particular?—ah dear fir, faid Jofeph, I muft tell you, though I never

ver uttered it to mortal man before, the ftriking
refemblance this young man bears to my dear
lord, the ftrange diflike his reputed father took
to him, his gentle manners, his generous heart,
his noble qualities fo uncommon in thofe of his
birth and breeding, the found of his voice—
you may fmile at the ftrength of my fancy,
but I cannot put it out of my mind but that he
is my own mafter's fon.

At thefe words Edmund changed colour and
trembled, he clapped his hand upon his breaft
and looked up to heaven in filence, his dream
recurred to his memory, and ftruck upon his
heart.—he related it to his attentive auditors.
The ways of providence are wonderful, faid
Ofwald, if this be fo, heaven in its own time
will make it appear.

Here a filence of feveral minutes enfued,
when fuddenly they were awakened from their
reverie by a violent noife in the rooms underneath them.—it feemed like the clafhing of
arms, and fomething feemed to fall down with
violence

They ftarted, and Edmund rofe up with a
look full of refolution and intrepidity.—I am
called! faid he, I obey the call!—he took up
a lamp and went to the door that he had
opened the night before. Ofwald followed
with his rofary in his hand, and Jofeph laft
with trembling fteps.—the door opened with
eafe, and they defcended the ftairs in profound
filence.

The lower rooms anfwered exactly to thofe
above ; there were two parlours and a large
clofet.—they faw nothing remarkable in thefe
rooms, except two pictures that were turned
with

with their faces to the wall.—Joseph took the courage to turn them, these, said he, are the portraits of my late lord and lady.—father, look at this face, do you know who is like it. —I should think, said Oswald, it was done for Edmund; I am, said Edmund, struck with the resemblance myself, but let us go on, I feel myself inspired with unusual courage, let us open the closet door.—Oswald stopped him short, take heed, said he, lest the wind of the door put out the lamp.—I will open this door, he attempted it without success, Joseph did the same, but to no purpose; Edmund gave the lamp to Joseph, he approached the door, tried the key, and it gave way to his hand in a moment.—this adventure belongs, said he, to me only, that is plain, bring the lamp forward.—Oswald repeated the paternoster, in which they all joined, and then entered the closet.

The first thing that presented itself to their view was a compleat suit of armour that seemed to have fallen down on an heap.——behold, said Edmund! this made the noise we heard above; they took it up and examined it piece by piece; the inside of the breast-plate was stained with blood.—see here, said Edmund, what think you of this?—'tis my lord's armour, said Joseph, I know it well, here has been bloody work in this closet; coming forward he stumbled over something, it was a ring with the arms of Lovel engraven upon it. —this is my lord's ring, said Joseph, I have seen him wear it, I give it to you, sir, as the right owner, and most religiously do I believe you his son. Heaven only knows that, said

G   Edmund,

Edmund, and if it permits, I will know who was my father before I am a day older.—while he was ſpeaking he ſhifted his ground, and perceived that the boards roſe up on the other ſide the cloſet; upon farther examination they found that the whole floor was looſe, and a table that ſtood over them concealed the circumſtance from a caſual obſerver.—I perceive, ſaid Oſwald, that ſome great diſcovery is at hand.—God defend us! ſaid Edmund, but I verily believe that the perſon that owned this armour lies buried under us.—upon this a diſmal hollow groan was heard as if from underneath.—a ſolemn ſilence enſued, and marks of fear were viſible upon all three, the groan was thrice heard, Oſwald made ſigns for them to kneel, and he prayed audibly, that heaven would direct them how to act, he alſo prayed for the ſoul of the departed, that it might reſt in peace; after this he aroſe, but Edmund continued kneeling, he vowed ſolemnly to devote himſelf to the diſcovery of this ſecret, and the avenging the death of the perſon there buried; he then roſe up; it would be to no purpoſe for us to examine further, now when I am properly authorized I will have this place opened, I truſt that time is not far off.—I believe it, ſaid Oſwald, you are deſigned by heaven to be its inſtrument in bringing this deed of darkneſs to light; we are your creatures, only tell us what you would have us do, and we are ready to obey your commands.—I only demand your ſilence, ſaid Edmund, till I call for your evidence, and then you muſt ſpeak all you know, and all you ſuſpect.—oh, ſaid Joſeph, that I may but live to ſee that day,

day, and I fhall have lived long enough!——
come, faid Edmund, let us return up ftairs,
and we will confult further how I fhall proceed, and fo faying he went out of the clofet
and they followed him, he locked the door
and took the key out; I will keep this, faid
he, till I have power to ufe it to purpofe, left
any one fhould prefume to pry into the fecret
of this clofet, I will always carry it about me,
to remind me of what I have undertaken.

Upon this they all returned up ftairs into the
bed chamber, all was ftill and they heard nothing more to difturb them.—how, faid Edmund, is it poffible that I fhould be the fon of
lord Lovel? for however circumftances have
feemed to encourage fuch a notion, what reafon have I to believe it?—I am ftrangely puz-
zled about it, faid Ofwald.—it feems unlikely
that fo good a man as lord Lovel fhould corrupt the wife of a peafant his vaffal, and efpecially being fo lately married to a lady with
whom he was paffionately in love.—hold there,
faid Jofeph, my lord was incapable of fuch an
action, if mafter Edmund is the fon of my
lord, he is alfo the fon of my lady.—how can
that be, faid Edmund?—I don't know how,
faid Jofeph, but there is a perfon who can tell
if fhe will; I mean Margery Twyford, who
calls herfelf your mother.—you meet my
thoughts, faid Edmund, I had refolved before
you fpoke to vifit her, and to interrogate her
on the fubject, I will afk my lord's permiffion
to go this very day.—that is right, faid Ofwald,
but be cautious and prudent in your enquiries.
—if you, faid Edmund, would bear my company I fhould do better, fhe might think her-

felf

felf obliged to anfwer your queftions, and being lefs interefted in the event, you would be
more difcreet in your interrogations.—that I
will moft readily, faid he, and I will afk my
lord's permiffion for us both.—this point is
well determined, faid Jofeph, I am impatient
for the refult, and I believe my feet will carry
me to meet you whether I confent or not.—
I am as impatient as you, faid Ofwald, but
let us be filent as the grave, and let not a
word or look indicate any thing knowing or
myfterious.

The day light began to dawn upon their
conference, and Edmund obferving it, begged
his friends to withdraw in filence.—they did
fo, and left Edmund to his own rec llections.
His thoughts were too much employed for
fleep to approach him, he threw himfelf upon
the bed, and lay meditating how he fhould
proceed ; a thoufand fchemes were offered and
rejected, but he refolved at all events to leave
baron Fitz-Owen's family the firft opportunity
that offered.

He was fummoned as before to attend my
lord at breakfaft, during which, he was filent, abfent and referved.—my lord obferved
it, and rallied him, enquiring how he had
fpent the night.—in reflecting upon my fituation, my lord, and in laying plans for my future conduct. Ofwald took the hint and afked
permiffion to vifit Edmund's mother in his
company, and acquaint her with his intentions
of leaving the country foon. He confented
freely, but feemed unrefolved about Edmund's
departure.

They

They set out directly, and Edmund went
hastily to old Twyford's cottage, and declared
that every field seemed a mile to him.—re-
strain your warmth my son, said Ofwald, com-
pose your mind and recover your breath before you enter upon a bufnefs of such confequence. Margery met them at the door, and
asked Edmund what wind blew him thither?
is it so very surprizing, said he, that I should
visit my parents? yes it is, said she, confider-
ing the treatment you have met with from us,
but since Andrew is not in the house I may
say I am glad to see you; Lord blefs you what
a fine youth you be grown! 'tis a long time
since I saw you, but that is not my fault, many
a crofs word and many a blow have I had on
your account, but I may now venture to embrace my dear child. Edmund came forward
and embraced her fervently, the starting tears
on both sides evinced their affection; and why,
said he, should my father forbid you to embrace your child, what have I ever done to
deserve his hatred? nothing my dear boy, you
were always good and tender hearted, and deferved the love of every body. It is not common, said Edmund, for a parent to hate his first
born son without his having deferved it.—that is
true, said Ofwald, it is uncommon, it is un-
natural, nay I am of opinion it is almost im-
poflible. I am so convinced of this truth, that
I believe the man who thus hates and abuses
Edmund, cannot be his father. In faying this
he obferved her countenance attentively, she
changed colour apparently; come, said he,
let us fit down, and do you Margery anfwer
to what I have faid? blefled virgin, faid Mar-

gery,

gery, what does your reverence mean, what
do you fufpect? I fufpect, faid he, that Edmund
is not the fon of Andrew your hufband. Lord
blefs me, faid fhe, what is it you do fufpect?
—do not evade my queftion woman! I am
come here by authority to examine you upon
this point. The woman trembled every joint,
would to heaven, faid fhe, that Andrew was
at home! it is much better as it is, faid Ofwald,
you are the perfon we are to examine. Oh,
father, faid fhe, do you think that I—that I—
that I am to blame in this matter? what have I
done?—do you, fir, faid he, afk your own
queftions; upon this Edmuud threw himfelf
at her feet, and embraced her knees.—oh my
mother, faid he, for as fuch my heart owns
you, tell me for the love of heaven! tell me
who was my father?—gracious heaven! faid
fhe, what will become of me?—woman, faid
Ofwald, confefs the truth or you fhall be
compelled to do it; by whom had you this
youth?—who I, faid fhe, I had him! no father I am not guilty of the black crime of
adultery, God he knows my innocence, I am
not worthy to be the mother of fuch a fweet
youth as that is.—you are not his mother then,
nor Andrew his father?—oh what fhall I do
faid Margery, Andrew will be the death of
me!—no he fhall not, faid Edmund, you fhall
be protected and rewarded for the difcovery.
Goody, faid Ofwald, confefs the whole truth
and I will protect you from harm and from
blame, you may be the means of making
Edmund's fortune, in which cafe he will certainly provide for you; on the other hand, by
an obftinate filence you will deprive yourfelf
of

of all advantages you might receive from the
difcovery, and befide, you will foon be examined
in a different manner, and be obliged to confefs all you know, and nobody will thank
you for it.—ah, faid fhe, but Andrew beat
me the laft time I fpoke to Edmund, and told
me he would break every bone in my fkin if
ever I fpoke to him again.—he knows it then,
faid Ofwald? he know it, Lord he'p you, it
was all his own doing.—tell us then, aid
Ofwald, for Andrew fhall never know it, till
it is out of his power to punifh you.—'tis a
long ftory, faid fhe, and cannot be told in
a few words.—it will never be told at this
rate, faid he, fit down and begin it inftantly.—
my fate depends upon your words, faid Edmund,
—my foul is impatient of the fufpence! if ever
you loved me and cherifhed me, fhow it now,
and tell while I have breath to afk it.

He fat in extreme agitation of mind, his
words and actions were equally expreffive of
his inward emotions.—I will, faid fhe, but I
muft try to recollect all the circumftances.
You muft know young man, that you are juft
one and twenty years of age.—on what day
was he born, faid Ofwald.—the day before
yefterday, faid fhe, the 21ft. of September.—
a remarkable æra, faid he.—'tis fo indeed,
faid Edmund, oh that night! that apartment!
—be filent, faid Ofwald, and do you Margery
begin your ftory.

I will, faid fhe, juft one and twenty years
ago, on that very day, I loft my firft born fon,
I got a hurt by over-reaching myfelf when I
was near my time, and fo the poor child died;
and fo as I was fitting all alone, and very melancholy,

lancholy, Andrew came home from work.—
fee Margery, faid he, I have brought you a
child inſtead of that you have loſt; ſo he gave
me a bundle as I thought, but ſure enough it
was a child, a poor helpleſs babe juſt born,
and only rolled up in a fine handkerchief, and
over that a rich velvet-cloak trimmed with
gold lace.—and where did you find this, ſaid
I.—upon the foot bridge, ſays he, juſt below
the clay field; this child, ſaid he, belongs to
ſome great folk, and perhaps it may be enquired after one day and may make our fortunes; take care of it, ſaid he, and bring it
up as if it was your own   The poor infant
was cold, and it cried, and looked up at me
ſo pitifully, that I loved it; beſide my milk
was troubleſome to me, and I was glad to be
eaſed of it, ſo I gave it the breaſt, and from
that hour I loved the child as if it were my
own, and ſo I do ſtill if I dared to own it.——
·and is this all you know of Edmund's birth,
ſaid Oſwald.—no not all, ſaid Margery, but
pray look out and ſee whether Andrew is coming, for I am all over in a twitter.—he is not,
ſaid Oſwald, go on I befeech you!——this happened, ſaid ſhe, as I told you on the 21ſt. on
the morrow my Andrew went out early to
work, along with one Robin Rouſe, our neighbour, they ha . not been gone above an hour
when they both came back ſeemingly very
much frightened; ſays Andrew, go you Robin
and borrow a pick-axe at neighbour Styles's.
—what is the matter now, ſaid I?——matter
enough, quoth Andrew! we may come to be
hanged perhaps, as many an innocent man
have before us.—tell me what is the matter,
                                                    ſaid

said I? I will, said he, but if ever you open your mouth about it, woe be to you! I never will, said I, but he made me swear by all the blessed saints in the calendar; and then he told me, that as Robin and he were going over the foot bridge, where he found the child the evening before, they saw something floating upon the water, so they followed it, till it stuck against a stake, and found it to be the dead body of a woman: as sure as you are alive Madge, said he, this was the mother of the child I brought home.——merciful God, said Edmund! am I the child of that hapless mother?—be composed, said Oswald, proceed, good woman, the time is precious.—and so, said she, Andrew told me they dragged the body out of the river, and it was richly dressed, and must be somebody of consequence.—I suppose, said he, when the poor lady had taken care of her child, she went to find some help, and the night being dark her foot slipped and she fell into the river and was drowned.

Lord have mercy, said Robin, what shall we do with the dead body, we may be taken up for the murther, what had we to do to meddle with it?—ay, but, says Andrew, we must have something to do with it now, and our wisest way is to bury it.—Robin was sadly frightened, but at last they agreed to carry it into the wood and bury it there; so they came home for a pick-axe and shovel.—well, said I Andrew, but will you bury all the rich clothes you speak of?—why, said he, it would be both a sin and a shame to strip the dead.—so it would, said I, but I will give you a sheet to wrap the body in, and you may take off her
upper

upper garments, and any thing of value, but do not ſtrip her to the ſkin for any thing,——well ſaid wench! ſaid he, I will do as you ſay, ſo I fetched a ſheet and by that time Robin was come back, and away they went together.

They did not come back again till noon, and then they ſat down and ate a morſel together.—ſays Andrew, now we may ſet down and eat in peace.—ay, ſays Robin, and ſleep in peace too, for we have done no harm.—no to be ſure, ſaid I, but yet I am much concerned that the poor lady had not chriſtian burial.—never trouble thyſelf about that, ſaid Andrew, we have done the beſt we could for her, but let us ſee what we have got in our bags, we muſt divide them; ſo they opened their bags and took out a fine gown and a pair of rich ſhoes, but beſides theſe, there was a fine necklace with a golden locket and a pair of earings.—ſays Andrew, and winked at me, I will have theſe, and you may take the reſt.—Robin ſaid he was ſatisfied, and ſo he went his way; when he was gone, here you fool, ſays Andrew, take theſe and keep them as ſafe as the bud of your eye, if ever young maſter is found, theſe will make our fortune.—and have you them now, ſaid Oſwald.—yes that I have, anſwered ſhe, Andrew would have ſold them long ago, but I always put him off it.—heaven be praiſed, ſaid Edmund!—huſh, ſaid Oſwald, let us not loſe time, proceed goody!—nay ſaid Margery, I have not much more to ſay.—we looked every day to hear ſome enquiries after the child, but nothing paſſed, nobody was miſſing.
——did

—did nobody of note die about that time, said Oſwald.—why yes, ſaid Margery, the widow lady Lovel died that ſame week, by the ſame token Andrew went to the funeral and brought home a 'ſcutcheon, which I keep unto this day.—very well, go on.—my huſband behaved well enough to the boy till ſuch time as he had two or three children of his own, and then he began to grumble, and ſay it was hard to maintain other folks children, when he found it hard enough to keep his own. I loved the boy quite as well as my own; often and often have I pacified Andrew, and made him to hope that he ſhould one day or other be paid for his trouble, but at laſt he grew out of patience, and gave over all hopes of that kind.

As Edmund grew up, he grew ſickly and tender, and could not bear hard labour, and that was another reaſon why my huſband could not bear with him.—if, quoth he, the boy could earn his living I did not care, but I muſt bear all the expence. There came an old pilgrim into our parts, he was a ſcholar and had been a ſoldier, and he taught Edmund to read, then he told him hiſtories of wars, and knights, and lords, and great men, and Edmund took ſuch delight in hearing him, that he would not take to any thing elſe.

To be ſure Edwin was a pleaſant compani-on, he would tell old ſtories and ſing old ſongs that one could have ſat all night to hear him; but as I was a ſaying, Edmund grew more and more fond of reading and lets of work; however he would run of errands and do many hand turns for the neighbours, and he was ſo courteous a lad that people took notice of him.

Andrew

Andrew once catched him alone reading, and then told him, that if he did not find some way to earn his bread, he would turn him out of doors in a very short time, and so he would have done sure enough, if my lord Fitz-Owen had not taken him into his service just in the nick.

Very well goody, said Oswald, you have told your story very well, I am glad for Edmund's fake, that you can do it properly; but now, can you keep a secret?—why ant please your reverence, I think I have showed you that I can.—but can you keep it from your husband? —aye, said she, surely I can, for I dare not tell it him —that is a good security, said he, but I must have a better.——you must swear upon this book not to disclose any thing that has passed between us three, till we desire you to do it, be assured you will soon be called upon for this purpose, Edmund's birth is near the discovery, he is the son of parents of high degree, and it will be in his power to make your fortune when he takes possession of his own.

Holy virgin! what is it you tell me?—how you rejoice me to hear, that what I have so long prayed for will come to pass!—she took the oath required, saying after Oswald.—now, said he, go and fetch the tokens you have mentioned.

When she was gone, Edmund's passions long suppressed, broke out in tears and exclamations, he kneeled down, and with his hands clasped together, returned thanks to heaven for the discovery; Oswald begged him to be composed, left Margery should perceive his agitation

agitation and misconstrue the cause.—she soon returned with the necklace and earings; they were pearls of great value, and the necklace had a locket on which the cypher of Lovel was engraved.—this, said Oswald, is indeed a proof of consequence, keep it sir, for it belongs to you.—must he take it away, said she? certainly, said he, we can do nothing without it? but if Andrew should ask for it, you must put him off it for the present, and hereafter he will find his account in it.—Margery consented reluctantly to part with the jewels, and after some further conversation they took leave of her.—Edmund embraced her affectionately.—I thank you with my whole heart, said he, for all your goodness to me! though I confess I never felt much regard for your husband, for you I had always the tender affection of a son; you will, I trust, give your evidence in my behalf when called upon, and I hope it will one day be in my power to reward your kindness, in that case I will own you as my foster-mother and you shall always be treated as such.——Margery wept.—the Lord grant it, said she; and I pray him to have you in his holy keeping.—farewell my dear child! Oswald desired them to separate for fear of intrusion, and they returned to the castle. Margery stood at the door of her cottage looking every way to see if the coast was clear.

Now, sir, said Oswald, I congratulate you as the son of lord and lady Lovel! the proofs are strong and indisputable.—to us they are so, said Edmund, but how shall we make them so to others? and what are we to think of the funeral of lady Lovel?—as of a fiction, said

H Oswald,

Ofwald, the work of the prefent lord, to fecure his title and fortune.—and what means can we ufe to difpofefs him, faid Edmund, he is not a man for a poor youth like me to contend with?—doubt not, faid Ofwald, but heaven, who has evidently conducted you by the hand thus far, will compleat its own work, for my part I can only wonder and adore!—give me your advice then, faid Edmund, for heaven affifts us by natural means.

It feems to me, faid Ofwald, that your firft ftep muft be to make a friend of fome great man, of confequence enough to efpoufe your caufe, and to get this affair examined into by authority.—Edmund ftarted and croffed himfelf.—he fuddenly exclaimed, a friend!—yes, I have a friend! a powerful one too, one fent by heaven to be my protector, but whom I have too long neglected.—who can that be? faid Ofwald.—who fhould it be, faid Edmund, but that good fir Philip Harclay, the chofen friend of him, whom I fhall from henceforward call my father.—'tis true indeed, faid Ofwald, and this is a frefh proof of what I before obferved, that heaven affifts you, and will compleat its own work.—I think fo myfelf, faid Edmund, and rely upon its direction, I have already determined on my future conduct which I will communicate to you. My firft ftep fhall be to leave the caftle, my lord has this day given me a horfe, upon which I purpofe to fet out this very night, without the knowledge of any of the family, I will go to fir Philip Harclay, I will throw myfelf at his feet, relate my ftrange ftory, and implore his protection, and with him I will confult on the

most

most proper way of bringing this murtherer to publick justice, and I will be guided by his advice and direction in every thing.—nothing can be better, said Oswald, than what you propose, but give me leave to offer an addition to your scheme ; you shall set off in the dead of night as you intend, Joseph and I will favour your departure in such a manner as to throw a mystery over the circumstances of it ; your disappearing at such a time from the haunted apartment, will terrify and confound all the family, they will puzzle themselves in vain to account for it, and they will be afraid to pry into the secrets of that place.

You say well, and I approve your addition, said Edmund, and suppose there was a letter written in a mysterious manner, and dropt in my lord's way, or sent to him afterwards, it would forward our design and frighten them away from that apartment.—that shall be my care, said Oswald, and I will warrant you that they will not find themselves disposed to inhabit it presently.—but how shall I leave my dear friend mr. William without a word of notice of this separation ?—I have thought of that too, said Oswald, and I will manage so as to acquaint him with it, in such a manner as he shall think out of the common course of things, and shall make him wonder and be silent.—how will you do that, said Edmund?—I will tell you hereafter, said Oswald, for here comes old Joseph to meet us.

He came indeed as fast as his age would permit him, as soon as he was within hearing he asked them what news?—they related all that had passed at Twyford's cottage, he heard

H 2   them

them with the greateſt eagerneſs of attention, and as ſoon as they came to the great event. —I knew it!—I knew it!—exclaimed Joſeph, I was ſure it would prove ſo!—thank God for it!—but I will be the firſt to acknowledge my young lord, and I will live and die his faith-ful ſervant!—here Joſeph attempted to kneel to him, but Edmund prevented him with a warm embrace,—my friend, my dear friend! ſaid he, I cannot ſuffer a man of your age to kneel to me, are you not one of my beſt and trueſt friends, I will ever remember your dif-intereſted affection for me, and if heaven re-ſtores me to my rights, it ſhall be one of my firſt cares to render your old age eaſy and happy. —Joſeph wept over him, and it was ſome time before he could utter a word.

Oſwald gave them both time to recover their emotion, by acquainting Joſeph with Edmund's ſcheme for his departure.—Joſeph wiped his eyes and ſpoke.—I have thought of ſomething that will be both agreeable and uſe-ful to my dear maſter.—John Wyatt, ſir Philip Harclay's ſervant, is now upon a viſit at his father's, I have heard that he goes home ſoon, now he would be both a guide and companion on the way.—that is indeed a happy circum-ſtance, ſaid Edmund, but how ſhall we know certainly the time of his departure?—why ſir I will go to him and enquire, and bring you word directly.—do ſo, ſaid Edmund, and you will oblige me greatly.—but ſir, ſaid Oſwald, I think it will be beſt not to let John Wyatt know who is to be his companion. only let Joſeph tell him that a gentleman is going to viſit his maſter, and if poſſible prevail upon
him

him to set out this night.—do so, my good friend, said Edmund, and tell him further, that this person has business of great consequence to communicate to his master, and cannot delay his journey on any account.—I will do this you may depend, said Joseph, and acquaint you with my success as soon as possible, but sir you must not go without a guide at any rate.—I trust I shall not, said Edmund, though I go alone, he that has received such a call as I have, can want no other, nor fear any danger.

They conversed on these points till they drew near the castle, when Joseph left them to go on his errand, and Edmund attended his lord at dinner.—the baron observed that he was silent and reserved, the conversation languished on both sides.—as soon as dinner was ended, Edmund asked permission to go up into his own apartment, where he packed up some necessaries, and made a hasty preparation for his departure.

Afterwards he walked into the garden, revolving in his mind the peculiarity of his situation, and the uncertainty of his future prospects.—lost in thought, he walked to and fro in a covered walk, with his arms croft and his eyes cast down, without perceiving that he was observed by two females who stood at a distance watching his motions.—it was the lady Emma and her attendant who were thus engaged, at length he lifted up his eyes and saw them; he stood still and was irresolute whether to advance or retire, they approached him; and as they drew near, said Emma spoke. You have been so wrapt in meditation, Edmund,

that

that I am apprehenfive of fome new vexation
that I am yet a ftranger to, would it were my
power to leffen thofe you have already! but
tell me if I guefs truly?—he ftood ftill irrefo-
lute, he anfwered with hefitation.—oh lady—
I am—I am grieved, I am concerned to be the
caufe of fo much confufion in this noble family, to which I am fo much indebted.—I fee
no way to leffen thefe evils but to remove the
caufe of them.—meaning yourfelf, faid fhe?—
certainly madam, and I was meditating on
my' departure —but, faid fhe, by your departure you will not remove the caufe.—how
fo madam?—becaufe you are not the caufe,
but thofe you will leave behind you.—lady
Emma!—how can you affect this ignorance,
Edmund, you know well enough it is that
odious Wenlock, your enemy and my averfion,
that has caufed all this mifchief among us,
and will much more if he is not removed.—
this madam is a fubject that it becomes me
to be filent upon; mr. Wenlock is your kinfman, he is not my friend, and for that reafon I ought not to fpeak againft him, nor you
to hear it from me; if he has ufed me ill, I am
recompenced by the generous treatment of
my lord your father, who is all that is great
and good, he has allowed me to juftify myfelf
to him, and he has reftored me to his good
opinion, which I prize among the beft gifts
of heaven; your amiable brother William
thinks well of me, and his efteem is infinitely
dear to me, and you, excellent lady, permit
me to hope that you honour with your good
opinion; are not thefe ample amends for the
ill will mr. Wenlock bears me?—my opinion
of

of you, Edmund, faid fhe, is fixed and fettled, it is not founded upon events of yefte 'ay, but upon long knowledge and experience upon your whole conduct and character.—you honour me lady ! continue to think well of me, it will excite me to deferve it ; when I am far diftant from this place, the remembrance of your goodnefs. will be a cordial to my heart, but why will you leave us, Edmund ? ftay and defeat the defigns ot your enemy, you fhall have my wifhes and affiftance.—pardon me, madam, that is among the things I cannot do, even if it were in my power, which it is not. Mr. Wenlock loves you lady, and if he is fo unhappy as to be your averfion, that is a punifhment fevere enough.—for the reft, I may be unfortunate by the wickednefs of others, but if I am unworthy it muft be by my own fault.—fo then you think it is an unworthy action to oppofe mr. Wenlock, very well fir, then I fuppofe you wifh him fuccefs, you wifh that I may be married to him?—I madam, faid Edmund, confufed; what am I that I fhould give my opinion on an affair of fo much confequence; you diftrefs me by the queftion; may you be happy ! may you enjoy your own wifhes! he fighed, he turned away, fhe called him back, he trembled and kept filence.

. She feemed to enjoy his confufion, fhe was cruel enough to repeat the queftion.—tell me, Edmund, and truly, do you wifh to fee me give my hand to Wenlock? I infift upon your anfwer.—all on a fudden he recovered both his voice and courage ; he ftepped forward, his perfon erect, his countenance affured, his

voice

voice refolute and intrepid.—fince lady Emma
infifts upon my anfwer, fince fhe avows a
diflike to Wenlock, fince fhe condefcends to
afk my opinion, I will tell her my thoughts,
my wifhes.—the fair Emma now trembled
in her turn, fhe blufhed, looked down, and
was afhamed to have fpoken fo freely.——
Edmund went on, my moft ardent wifhes are
that the fair Emma may referve her heart and
hand till a certain perfon, a friend of mine, is
at liberty to folicit them, whofe utmoft ambition is, firft to deferve, and then to obtain
them.—your friend fir! faid lady Emma, her
brow clouded, her eye difdainful.—Edmund
proceeded ; my friend is fo particularly cir-
cumftanced that he cannot at prefent with
propriety afk for lady Emma's favour, but as
foon as he has gained a caufe that is yet in fufpence, he will openly declare his pretenfions,
and if he is unfuccefsful he will condemn himfelf to eternal filence.—lady Emma knew not
what to think of this declaration, fhe hoped,
fhe feared, fhe meditated, but her attention
was too ftrongly excited to be fatisfied without
fome gratification ; after a paufe fhe perfued
the fubject.—and this friend of yours fir, of
what degree and fortune is he?—Edmund
fmiled, but commanding his emotion, he replied, his birth is noble, his degree and fortune uncertain.—her countenance fell, fhe
fighed, he proceeded.—it is utterly impoffible,
faid he, for any man of inferior degree to afpire to lady Emma's favour, her noble birth,
the dignity of her beauty and virtues, muft
awe and keep at their proper diftance, all men
of inferior degree and merit, they may admire,
                                           they

they may revere, but they muſt not preſume to approach too near, leſt their preſumption ſhould meet with its puniſhment.—well, ſir, ſaid ſhe, ſuddenly, and ſo this friend of yours. has commiſſioned you to ſpeak in his behalf? —he has madam.—then I muſt tell you that I think his aſſurance very great, and yours not much leſs.—I am ſorry for that madam.—tell him that I ſhall reſerve my heart and hand for the man to whom my father ſhall bid me give them.—very well lady, I am certain my lord loves you too well to diſpoſe of them againſt your inclination.—how do you know that ſir, but tell him that the man that hopes for my favour muſt apply to my lord for his. —that is my friend's intention, his reſolution I ſhould ſay, as ſoon as he can do it with propriety, and I accept your permiſſion for him to do ſo.—my permiſſion did you ſay? I am aſtoniſhed at your aſſurance! tell me no more of your friend, but perhaps you are pleading for Wenlock all this time, it is all one to me, only ſay no more.—are you offended with me madam?—no matter ſir.—yes it is, I am ſurprized at you! I am ſurprized at my own temerity, but forgive me.—it does not ſignify, good bye ty'e ſir.—dont leave me in anger madam, I cannot bear that, perhaps I may not ſee you again preſently?—he looked afflicted, ſhe turned back.—I do forgive you, Edmund, I was concerned for you, but it ſeems you are more concerned for every body than yourſelf.—ſhe ſighed, farewell, ſaid ſhe!—Edmund gazed on her with tenderneſs, he approached her, he juſt touched her hand, his heart was riſing to his lips, but he recollected

his

his situation, he checked himself immediately, he retired back, he sighed deeply, bowed low, and retired hastily.

The lady turned into another walk, and he reached the house first, and went up again to his chamber, threw himself upon his knees, prayed for a thousand blessings upon every one of the family of his benefactor, and involuntarily wept at mentioning the name of the charming Emma, whom he was about to leave abruptly, and perhaps for ever.—he composed himself and once again attended the baron, wished him a good night, and withdrew to his chamber, till he was called to go again to the haunted apartment.

He came down equipped for his journey, and went hastily for fear of observation ; he paid his customary devotions, and soon after Ofwald tapped at the door ; they conferred together upon the interesting subject that engroffed their attention, until Joseph came to them ; he brought the rest of Edmund's baggage, and some refreshment for him before he set out.—Edmund promised to give them the earliest information of his situation and success ; at the hour of twelve they heard the same groans as the night before in the lower apartment, but being somewhat familiarized to it, they were not so strongly affected ; Ofwald crossed himself, and prayed for the departed soul, he also prayed for Edmund, and recommended him to the divine protection ; he then arose and embraced that young man, who also took a tender leave of his friend Joseph ; they then went with silence and caution through a long gallery, they descended the stairs in the same

same manner, they crossed the hall in profound silence, and hardly dared to breathe lest they should be overheard; they found some difficulty in opening one of the folding doors, which at last they accomplished; they were again in jeopardy at the outward gate, at length they conveyed him safely into the stables, there they again embraced him, and prayed for his prosperity.

. He then mounted his horse and set forward to Wyatt's cottage; he hallowed at the door and was answered from within; in a few minutes John came out to him; what is it you, master Edmund?—hush, said he, not a word of who I am, I go upon private business, and would not wish to be known.—if you will go forward sir, I will soon overtake you; he did so, and they pursued their journey to the north. In the mean time Oswald and Joseph returned in silence into the house, they retired to their respective apartments without hearing or being heard by any one.

.. About the dawn of day Oswald intended to lay his pacquets in the way of those they were addressed to, after much contrivance he determined to take a bold step, and if he were discovered, to frame some excuse. Encouraged by his late success, he went on tip-toe into master William's chamber, placed a letter upon his pillow, and withdrew unheard.——— exulting in his heart, he attempted the baron's apartment, but found it fastened within; finding this scheme frustrated, he waited till the hour the baron was expected down to breakfast, and laid the letter and the key of the haunted apartment upon the table.

Soon

Soon after he saw the baron enter the breakfast room, he got out of sight, but staid within call, preparing himself for a summons. The baron sat down to breakfast, he saw a letter directed to himself, he opened it, and to his great surprise, read as follows.

" The guardian of the haunted apart-
" ment to baron Fitz-Owen.   To thee I remit
" the key of my charge, until the right owner
" shall come, who will both discover and a-
" venge my wrongs ; then woe be to the
" guilty! but let the innocent rest in peace.
" In the mean time let none presume to ex-
" plore the secrets of my apartment, lest they
" suffer for their temerity."

The baron was struck with amazement at the letter, he took up the key, examined it, then laid it down and took up the letter ; he was in such confusion of thought, he knew not what to do or say for several minutes, at length he called his servants about him, the first question he asked was, where is Edmund? —they could not tell.—has he been called?— yes my lord, but nobody answered, and the key was not in the door.—where is Joseph? —gone into the stables.—where is father Os- wald?—in his study.—seek him, and desire him to come hither.—by the time the baron had read the letter over again, he came.

He had been framing a steady countenance to answer to all interrogatories, as he came in he attentively observed the baron, whose features were in strong agitation; as soon as he saw Oswald, he spoke as one out of breath. —take that key, and read this letter!—he did so, shrugged up his shoulders and remained silent.

filent.—father, faid my lord, what think you of this letter? it is a very furprifing one.—the contents are alarming, where is Edmund?—I do not know.—has nobody feen him.—not that I know of.—call my fons, my kinfmen, my fervants!—they came in.—have any of you feen or heard of Edmund?—no was the anfwer.—father ftep up ftairs to my fons and kinfmen, and defire them to come down immediately.

Ofwald withdrew, and went firft to mr. William's chamber.—my dear fir, you muft come to my lord now directly, he has fomething extraordinary to communicate to you.—and fo have I father, fee what I have found upon my pillow!—pray fir read it to me before you fhow it to any body, my lord is alarmed too much already, and wants nothing to increafe his confternation.—William read his letter, while Ofwald looked as if he was an utter ftranger to the contents, which were thefe.

" Whatever may be heard or feen, let the " feal of friendfhip be upon thy lips; the pea- " fant Edmund is no more, but there ftill lives " a man who hopes to acknowledge and re- " pay the lord Fitz-Owen's generous care and " protection; to return his beloved William's " vowed affection, and to claim his friendfhip " on terms of equality."

What, faid William can this mean?—it is not eafy to fay, faid Ofwald.—can you tell what is the caufe of this alarm?—I can tell you nothing, but that my lord defires to fee you directly, pray make hafte down, I muft go up to your brothers and kinfmen, nobody knows what to think or believe.

I   Mafter

Mafter William went down ftairs, and father Ofwald went to the malecontents; as foon as he entered the outward door of their apartment, mr. Wenlock called out, here comes the friend, now for fome new propofal!——genltemen, faid Ofwald, my lord defires your company immediately in the breakfaft parlour.—what to meet your favourite Edmund I fuppofe? faid mr. Wenlock.—no fir.—what then is the matter, faid fir Robert?—fomething very extraordinary has happened, gentlemen, Edmund is not to be found, he difappeared from the haunted apartment, the key of which was conveyed to my lord in a ftrange manner, with a letter from an unknown hand; my lord is both furprized and concerned, and wifhes to have your opinion and advice on the occafion.—tell him, faid fir Robert, we will wait upon him immediately.

As Ofwald went away he heard Wenlock fay, fo Edmund is gone it is no matter how or whither.—another faid, I hope the ghoft has taken him out of the way.—the reft laughed at the conceit, as they followed Ofwald down ftairs.—they found the baron and his fon William commenting upon the key and the letter.—my lord gave them to fir Robert, who looked on them with marks of furprize and confufion.—the baron addreffed him.—is not this a very ftrange affair?—fon Robert, lay afide your ill humours, and behave to your father with the refpect and affection his tendernefs deferves from you, and give me your advice and opinion on this alarming fubject?—my lord, faid fir Robert, I am as much confounded as yourfelf,

felf, I can give no advice, let my coufins fee the letter, let us have their opinion.—they read it in turn, they were equally furprized, but when it came into Wenlock's hand, he paufed and meditated fome minutes, at length —I am indeed furprized, and ftill more concerned, to fee my lord and uncle the dupe of an artful contrivance, and if he will permit me I fhall endeavour to unriddle it, to the confufion of all that are concerned in it.—do fo, Dick, faid my lord, and you fhall have my thanks for it.—this letter, faid he, I imagine to be the contrivance of Edmund, or fome ingenious friend of his, to conceal fome defigns they have againft the peace of this family, which has been too often difturbed upon that rafcal's account.—but what end could be propofed by it? faid the baron.—why one part of the fcheme is to cover Edmund's departure, that is clear enough ; for the reft we can only guefs at it. —perhaps he may be hid up fomewhere in that apartment, from whence he may rufh out in the night, and either rob or murther us, or at leaft alarm and terrify the family.—the baron fmiled, you fhoot beyond the mark fir, and overfhoot yourfelf, as you have done before now, you fhow only your inveteracy againft that poor lad, whom you cannot mention with temper ; to what purpofe fhould he fhut himfelf up there, to be ftarved ?—ftarved ! no, no ! he has friends in this houfe, (looking at Ofwald) who will not fuffer him to want any thing ; thofe who have always magnified his virtues, and extenuated his faults, will lend a hand to help him in time of need, and perhaps to affift his ingenious contrivances.——

Ofwald

Ofwald fhrugged up his fhoulders and remained filent.—this is a ftrange fancy of yours, Dick, faid my lord, but I am willing to perfue it, firft to difcover what you drive at, and fecondly to fatisfy all that are here prefent of the truth or falfhood of it, that they may know what value to fet upon your fagacity hereafter. —let us all go over that apartment together, and let Jofeph be called to attend us thither; Ofwald offered to call him, but Wenlock ftopped him.—no father, faid he, you muft ftay with us, we want your ghoftly counfel and advice; Jofeph fhall have no private conference with you.—what mean you, faid Ofwald, to infinuate to my lord againft me or Jofeph? but your ill will fpares nobody, it will one day he known who is the difturber of the peace of this family, I wait for that time; and am filent.

Jofeph came, when he was told whither they were going, he looked hard at Ofwald. Wenlock obferved them.—lead the way father! faid he, and Jofeph fhall follow us.—— Ofwald fmiled.—we will go where heaven permits us, faid he,—alas!—the wifdom of man can neither haften nor retard its decrees.

'They followed the father up ftairs, and went directly to the haunted apartment.—the baron unlocked the door, he bid Jofeph open the fhutters and admit the day light, which had been excluded for many years.—they went over the rooms above ftairs, and then defcended the ftaircafe and through the lower rooms in the fame manner.—however they overlooked the clofet in which the fatal fecret was concealed.—the door was covered with
tapeftry

tapefty the fame as the room, and united fo
well that it feemed but one piece.—Wenlock
tauntingly defired father Ofwald to introduce
them to the ghoft.—the father in reply, afked
them where they fhould find Edmund? do
you think, faid he, that he lies hid in my pocket
or in Jofeph's.—'tis no matter, anfwered he,
thoughts are free.—my opinion of you fir,
faid he, is not founded upon thoughts, I judge
of men by their actions, a rule I believe it will
not fuit you to be tried by.—none of your in-
folent admonitions, father! faid he, this is
neither the time nor the place for them—that
is truer than you are aware of, fir, I meant
not to enter into the fubject juft now.—be filent, faid my lord.—I fhall enter into this fubject with you hereafter, then look you be prepared for it! in the mean time do you Dick
Wenlock anfwer to my queftions?—do you
think Edmund is concealed in this apartment?
—no fir.—do you think there is any myftery in
it?—no my lord.—is it haunted, think you?
—no, I think not.—fhould you be afraid to
try?—in what manner my lord?—why you
have fhown your wit upon the fubject, and I
mean to fhow your courage, you and Jack
Markham, your confident, fhall fleep here
three nights as Edmund has done before.—
fir, faid fir Robert, for what purpofe, I fhould
be glad to underftand why?—I have my reafons fir, as well as your kinfmen there.—no
reply firs! I infift upon being being obeyed in
this point; Jofeph let the beds be well aired,
and every thing made agreeable to the gentlemen; if there is any contrivance to impofe
upon me, they I am fure will have pleafure in

I 3   de-

detecting it, and if not, I shall obtain my end in making these rooms habitable.—Oswald come with me, and the rest may go where they list till dinner time.

The baron went with Oswald into the parlour.—now tell me, father, said he, do you disapprove what I have done?— quite the contrary my lord, said he, I entirely approve it. —but you do not know all my reasons for it; yesterday Edmund's behaviour was different from what I have ever seen it, he is naturally frank and open in all his ways, but he was silent, thoughtful, absent, he sighed deeply, and once I saw tears stand in his eyes; now I do suspect there is something uncommon in that apartment, that Edmund has discovered the secret, and fearing to disclose it, he is fled away from the house; as to this letter, perhaps he may have written it to hint that there is more than he dares reveal; I tremble at the hints contained in it, though I shall appear to make light of it; but I and mine are innocent, and if heaven discloses the guilt of others, I ought to adore and submit to its decrees.—that is prudently and piously resolved my lord, let us do our duty and leave events to heaven.—but father I have a further view in obliging my kinsman to sleep there, if any thing should appear to them, it is better that it should only be known to my own family; if there is nothing in it, I shall put to the proof, the courage and veracity of my two kinsmen, of whom I think very indifferently. —I mean shortly to enquire into many things I have heard lately to their disadvantage, and if I find them guilty, they shall not escape with

im-

impunity:—my lord, said Oswald, you judge like yourself, I wish you to make enquiry concerning them, and believe the result will be to their confusion, and your lordship will be enabled to re-establish the peace of your family.

During this conversation, Oswald was upon his guard, lest any thing should escape that might create suspicion.—he withdrew as soon as he could with decency, and left the baron meditating what all these things should mean, he feared there was some misfortune impending over his house, though he knew not from what cause.

He dined with his children and kinsmen, and strove to appear cheaful, but a gloom was perceivable through his deportment.—sir Robert was reserved and respectful.—mr. William was silent and attentive, the rest of the family dutifully assiduous to my lord, only Wenlock and Markham were sullen and chagrined.— the baron detained the young men the whole afternoon, he strove to amuse and to be amused, he showed the greatest affection and parental regard to his children, and endeavoured to conciliate their affections, and engage their gratitude by kindness.—Wenlock and Markham felt their courage abate as the night approached; at the hour of nine old Joseph came to conduct them to the haunted apartment, they took leave of their kinsmen and went up stairs with heavy hearts.

They found the chamber set in order for them, and a table spread with provision and good liquor to keep up their spirits.—it seems, said Wenlock, that your friend Edmund, was

obliged

obliged to you for his accommodations here.
—fir, faid Joseph, his accommodations were
bad enough the firft night, but afterwards they
were bettered by my lord's orders.—owing to
your officious cares, faid Wenlock, I own it,
faid Joseph, and I am not afhamed of it.——
are you not anxious to know what is become
of him, faid Markham.—not at all fir, I truft
he is in the beft protection, fo good a young
man as he is fate every where.—you fee coufin Jack, faid Wenlock, how this villain has
ftole the hearts of my uncle's fervants; I fuppofe this canting old fellow knows where he
is if the truth were known.—have you any
further comm:n ls for me, gentlemen, faid
the old man?—no not we.—then I am ordered
to attend my lord when you have done with
me.—go then about your bufinefs.—Joseph
went away, glad to be difmiffed.

What fhall we do coufin Jack, faid Wenlock, to pafs away the time? it is plaguy dull
fitting here.—dull enough, faid Markham, I
think the beft thing we can do is to go to bed
and fleep it away.—faith. fays Wenlock I am
in no difpofitiou to fleep!—who would have
thought the old man would have obliged us to
fpend the night here?—don't fay *us* I beg of
you, it was all your own doing.—I did not
intend he fhould have taken me at my word.
—then you fhould have fpoken more cautioufly.
—I have always been governed by you like a
fool as I am, you play the braggart, and I fuffer for it; but they begin to fee through your
fine fpun arts and contrivances, and I believe
you will meet with your deferts one day or
other.—what now!—do you mean to affront
me

me, Jack?—know that some are born to plan, others to execute, I am one of the former, thou of the latter.—know your friend, or—— or what, replied Markham? do you mean to threaten me?. if you do!—what then, said Wenlock.—why then I will try which of us two is the best man sir!—upon this Markham arose, and put himself into a posture of defence. —Wenlock perceiving he was serious in his anger, began to sooth him; he persuaded, he flattered, he promised great things if he would be composed.—Markham was sullen, uneasy, resentful; whenever he spoke it was to upbraid Wenlock with his treachery and falsehood.—Wenlock tried all his eloquence to get him into a good humour, but in vain, he threatened to acquaint his uncle with all that he knew, and to exculpate himself at the other's expence.—Wenlock began to find his choler rise, they were both almost choaked with rage, and at length they both rose with a resolution to fight.

As they stood with their fists clenched, on a sudden they were alarmed with a dismal groan from the room underneath; they stood like statues petrified by fear, yet listening with trembling expectation.—a second increased their consternation, and soon after a third compleated it; they staggered to a seat and sunk down upon it ready to faint; presently all the doors flew open, a pale glimmering light appeared at the door from the staircase, and a man in compleat armour entered the room; he stood with one hand extended, pointing to the outward door; they took the hint and crawled away as fast as fear would

let

let them ; they ftaggered along the gallery,
and from thence to the baron's apartment,
where Wenlock funk down in a fwoon, and
Markham had juft ftrength enough to knock at
the door.

The fervant who flept in the outward room
alarmed his lord, Markham cried out, for
heaven's fake let us in !—upon hearing his
voice, the door was opened, and Markham
approached his uncle in fuch an attitude of
fear, as excited a degree of it in the baron.—
he pointed to Wenlock, who was with fome
difficulty recovered from the fit he was fallen
into ; the fervant was terrified, he rung the
alarm bell, the fervants came running from
all parts to their lord's apartment ; the young
gentlemen came, and prefently all was confufion, and the terror was univerfal. Ofwald
who gueffed the bufinefs, was the only one
that could afked a queftion ; he afked feveral
times, what is the matter ?—Markham at laft
anfwered him.—we have feen the ghoft !——
all regard to fecrecy was at an end, the eccho
ran through the whole family.—they have
feen the ghoft !

The baron defired Ofwald to talk to the
young men, and endeavour to quiet the diftur-
bance.—he came forward, he comforted fome,
he rebuked others, he bad the fervants retire
into the outward room, the baron with his
fons and kinfmen remained in the bed chamber.—faid Ofwald, it is very unfortunate that
this affair fhould be made fo publick, furely
thefe young men might have related what they
had feen without alarming the whole family ;
I am very much concerned upon my lord's account.

count.—I thank you father, said the baron, but prudence was quite overthrown here, Wenlock was half dead, and Markham half distracted, the family were alarmed without my being able to prevent it,—but let us hear what these poor terrified creatures say?—Oswald demanded, what have you seen gentlemen?——the ghost, said Markham.—in what form did it appear?—a man in armour.—did it speak to you?—no.—what did it do to terrify you so much?—it stood at the farthest door, and pointed to the outward door, as if to have us leave the room; we did not wait for a second notice, but came away as fast as we could.—did it follow you?—no.—then you need not have raised such a disturbance.—Wenlock lifted up his head and spoke.—I believe father if you had been with us, you would not have stood upon ceremonies any more than we did.——I wish my lord would send you to parley with the ghost, for without doubt, you are better qualified than we.—my lord, said Oswald, I will go thither with your permission, I will see that every thing is safe, and bring the key back to you; perhaps this may help to dispel the fears that have been raised, at least I will try to do it.—I thank you father for your good offices, do as you please.

Oswald went into the outward room.—I am going, said he, to shut up the apartment, the young gentlemen have been more frightened than they had occasion for; I will try to account for it, which of you will go with me?—they all drew back, except Joseph, who offered to bear him company.—they went into the bed room in the haunted apartment, found

every

every thing quiet there.—they put out the fire, extinguished the lights, locked the door, and brought away the key.—as they returned I thought how it would be, said Joseph.—— hush! not a word, said Oswald, you find we are suspected of something, though they know not what.—wait till you are called upon, and then we will both speak to purpose; they carried the key to the baron.

· All is quiet in the apartment, said Oswald, as we can testify.—did you ask Joseph to go with you, said the baron, or did he offer himself?—my lord, I asked if any body would go with me, and they all declined it but he, I thought proper to have a witness beside myself, for whatever might be seen or heard.— Joseph, you was servant to the late lord Lovel, what kind of man was he?—a very comely man, please your lordship.—should you know him if you were to see him?—I cannot say, my lord.—would you have any objection to sleep a night in that apartment?—I beg,—I hope.—I beseech your lordship not to command me to do it!—you are then afraid, why did you offer yourself to go thither.—because I was not so much frightened as the rest.—I wish you would lay a night there, but I do not insist upon it.—my lord I am a poor ignorant old man, not fit for such an undertaking. —beside, if I should see the ghost, and if it should be the person of my master, and if it should tell me any thing, and bid me keep it secret, I should not dare to disclose it, and then what service should I do your lordship? that is true indeed, said the baron.

This

This fpeech, faid fir Robert, is both a fim-
ple and an artful one, you fee however, that
Jofeph is not a man for us to depend upon;
he regards the lord Lovel, though dead, more
than lord Fitz-Owen, living; he calls him his
mafter, and promifes to keep his fecrets.——
what fay you father, is the ghoft your mafter,
or your friend, are you under any obligation
to keep his fecrets?—fir, faid Ofwald, I anfwer as Jofeph does, I would fooner die than
difcover a fecret revealed in that manner.—I
thought as much, faid fir Robert, there is a
myftery in father Ofwald's behaviour that I
cannot comprehend.—do not reflect upon the
father, faid the baron, I have nothing to com-
plain of him for, perhaps the myftery may
be too foon explained; but let us not antici-
pate evils; Ofwald and Jofeph have fpoken
like good men, I am fatisfied with their anfwers; let us who are innocent reft in peace I
and let us endeavour to reftore peace in the
family, and do you father affift us?—with my
beft fervices, faid Ofwald.—he called the fervants in, let nothing be faid out of doors, faid
he, of what has lately paffed within, efpecially
in the eaft apartment; the young gentlemen
had not fo much room to be frightened as they
apprehended, a piece of furniture fell down
in the rooms underneath, which made the
noife that alarmed them fo much; but I can
certify that all things in the rooms are in
quiet, and there is nothing to fear; all of you
attend me in the chapel in an hour, do your
duties, put your truft in God, and obey your
lord, and you find every thing go right as it
ufed to do.

K They

They difperfed, the fun rofe, the day came on, and every thing went on in the ufual courfe; the fervants were not fo eafily fatisfied, they whifpered that fomething was wrong, and expected the time that fhould fet all right.—the mind of the baron was employed in meditating upon thefe circumftances that feemed to him the forerunners of fome great events; he fometimes thought of Edmund, he fighed for his expulfion, and lamented the uncertainty of his fate, but to his family he appeared eafy and fatisfied.

From the time of Edmund's departure the fair Emma had many uneafy hours, fhe wifhed to enquire after him, but feared to fhow any folicitude concerning him: one day when her brother William came into her apartment, fhe took courage to afk a queftion.—pray brother can you give any guefs what is become of Edmund?—no, faid he, (with a figh) why do you afk me?—becaufe my dear William, I fhould think if any body knew it, muft be you, and I thought he loved you too well to leave you in ignorance; but don't you think he left the caftle in a very ftrange manner?—I do my dear, there is a myftery in every circumftance of his departure; neverthelefs (I will truft you with a fecret) he did not leave the caftle without making a diftinction in my favour.——I thought fo, faid fhe.——but you might tell *me* what you know about him?—alas, my dear Emma! I know nothing, when I faw him laft he feemed a good deal affected, as if he were taking leave of me, and I had a foreboding that we parted for a longer time than ufual.— ah, fo had I, faid fhe, when he

parted

parted from me in the garden!—what leave
did he take of you Emma?—fhe blufhed and
hefitated to tell him all that paffed between
them; but he begged, perfuaded, infifted, and
at length under the ftrongeft injunctions of fecrecy, fhe told him all.—he faid that Edmund's
behaviour on that occafion was as myfterious
as the reft of his conduct; but now you have
revealed your fecret, you have a right to know
mine.—he then gave her the letter he found
upon his pillow, fhe read it with great emotion.—faint Winifred affift me! faid fhe.——
what can I think?—the peafant Edmund is no
more, but there lives one,—that is to my
thinking, Edmund lives, but is no peafant.—
go on my dear, faid William, I like yonr explanation.—nay, brother, I only guefs, but
what think you?—I believe we think alike in
more than one refpect, that he meant to recommend no other perfon than himfelf to your
favour, and that if he were indeed of noble
birth, I would prefer him to a prince for a
hufband to my Emma!—blefs me! faid fhe,
do you think it poffible that he fhould be of
birth or fortune?—it is hard to fay what is impoffible.—we have proof that the eaft apartment is haunted.—it was there that Edmund
was made acquainted with many fecrets, I
doubt not, and perhaps his own fate may be
involved in that of others.—I am confident
that what he faw and heard, there, was the
caufe of his departure; we muft wait with
patience the unravelling this intricate affair;
I believe I need not enjoin your fecrecy as to
what I have faid, your heart will be my fecurity.—what mean you brother?—don't affect

igno

Ignorance my dear, you love Edmund, so do I, it is nothing to be ashamed of, it would have been strange if a girl of your good sense had not distinguished a swan among a flock of geese.—dear William don't let a word of th s escape you, but you have taken a weight off my heart, you may depend that I will not dispose of my hand or heart till I know the end of this affair.—William smiled.—keep them for Edmund's *friend*, I shall rejoice to see him in a situation to ask them.—hush my brother! not a word more, I hear footsteps.——they were her eldest brother's, who came to ask mr. William to ride out with him, which finished the conference.

The fair Emma from this time assumed an air of satisfaction; and William frequently stole away from his companions to talk with his sister upon their favourite subject.

While these things passed at the castle of Lovel, Edmund and his companion John Wyat proceeded on their journey to sir Philip Harclay's seat, they conversed together on the way, and Edmund found him a man of understanding, though not improved by education, he also discovered that John loved his master and respected him even to veneration; from him he learned many particulars concerning that worthy knight.—Wyatt told him that sir Philip maintained twelve old soldiers who had been maimed and disabled in the wars, and had no provision made for them; also six old officers who had been unfortunate and were grown grey without preferment; he likewise mentioned the Greek gentleman, his master's captive and friend, as a

man

man eminent for valour and piety, but befide
thefe, faid Wyatt, there are many others who
eat of my mafter's bread and drink of his cup,
and who join in bleffings and prayers to heaven for their noble benefactor; his ears are
ever open to diftrefs, his hand to relieve it,
and he fhares in every good man's joys and
bleffings.—oh what a glorious character! faid
Edmund, how my heart throbs with wifhes to
imitate fuch a man! oh that I might refem-
ble him though at ever fo great a diftance!—
Edmund was never weary of hearing the actions
of this truly great man, nor Wyatt with relating them, and during three days journey,
there was but few paufes in their converfation.

The fourth day when they came within view
of the houfe, Edmund's heart began to raife
doubts of his reception.—if, faid he, fir Philip
fhould not receive me kindly, if he fhould re-
fent my long neglect, and difown my acquain-
tance, it would be no more than juftice.

He fent Wyatt before to notify his arrival
to fir Philip, while he waited at the gate, full
of doubts and anxieties concerning his reception, Wyatt was met and congratulated on his
return by moft of his fellow fervants; he
afked, where is my mafter?—in the parlour.—
are any ftrangers with him?—no, only his own
family.—then I will fhow myfelf to him.——
he prefented himfelf before fir Philip.—fo
John, faid he, you are welcome home! I hope
you left your parents and relations well?—all
well, thank God! and fend their humble duty
to your honour, and they pray for you every
day of their lives; I hope your honour is in
good health?—very well.—thank God for that!

K 3   but

but fir, I have fomething further to tell you, I have had a companion all the way home, a perfon who comes to wait on your honour on bufinefs of great coufequence, as he fays.——who is that John?—it is mafter Edmund Twyford from the caftle of Lovel.——young Edmund, fays fir Philip, furprized.—where is he?—at the gate fir.—why did you leave him there?—becaufe he bad me come before, and acquaint your honour that he waits your pleafure.—bring him hither, faid fir Philip, tell him I fhall be glad to fee him.

John made haft to deliver his meffage, and Edmund followed him in filence into fir Philip's prefence; he bowed low and kept at diftance. —fir Philip held out his hand and bad him approach.—as he drew near he was feized with an univerfal trembling; he kneeled down, took his hand, kiffed it, and preffed it to his heart in filence.

You are welcome young man! faid fir Philip, take courage and fpeak for yourfelf.—Edmund fighed deeply, he at length broke filence with difficulty.—I am come thus far, noble fir, to throw myfelf at your feet and implore your protection.—you are under God, my only reliance!—I receive you, faid fir Philip, with all my heart! your perfon is greatly improved fince I faw you laft, and I hope your mind is equally fo; I have heard a great character of you from fome that knew you in France; I remember the promife I made you long ago, and am ready now to fulfil it, upon condition that you have done nothing to difgrace the good opinion I formerly entertained of you, and am ready to ferve you in any thing confiftent

fiftent with my own honour.—Edmund killed
the hand that was extended to raife him.—
I accept your favour fir, upon this condition
only, and if ever you find me to impofe upon
your credulity, or increach on your goodnefs,
may you renounce me from that moment!—
enough, faid fir Philip, rife then and let me
embrace you, you are truly welcome!—oh noble fir, faid Edmund, I have a ftrange ftory to
tell you, but it muft be by ourfelves, with
only heaven to bear witnefs to what paffes
between us.—very well, faid fir Philip, I am
ready to hear you, but firft go and get fome
refrefhment after your journey, and then come
to me again, John Wyatt will attend you.—
I want no refrefhment, faid Edmund, and I
cannot eat or drink till I have told my bufinefs
to your honour.—well then, faid fir Philip,
come along with me, he took the youth by
the hand and led him into another parlour,
leaving his friends in great furprize, what this
young man's errand could be; John Wyatt
told them all that he knew relating to Edmund's birth, character and fituation.

When fir Philip had feated his young friend,
he liftened in filence to the furprizing tale he
had to tell him. Edmund told him briefly
the moft remarkable circumftances of his life,
from the time when he firft faw and liked
him, till his return from France, but from that
æra he related at large every thing that had
happened, recounting every interefting particular which was imprinted on his memory in
ftrong and lafting characters.—fir Philip grew
every moment more affected by the recital;
fometimes he clafped his hands together, he
lifted

lifed them up to heaven, he imote his breaft,
he fighed, he exclaimed aloud.—but when Edmund related h s dream, he breathed fhort, and
feemed to devour him with attention; when
he deicribed the fatal clofet he trembled,
fighed, iobbed, and was almoft fuffocated with
his agitations.—but when he related all that
paffed between his fuppofed mother and himfelf, and finally produced the jewels, the proofs
of his birth, and the death of his unfortunate
mother; he flew to him, he preffed him to
his bofom, he ftrove to fpeak, but fpeech was
for fome minutes denied; he wept aloud, and at
length his words found their way in broken
exclamations.—fon of my deareft friend !——
dear and precious relick of a noble houfe !—
child of providence !—the beloved of heaven!
—welcome! thrice welcome to my arms !—
to my heart !—I will be thy parent from henceforward, and thou fhalt be indeed my child,
my heir! my mind told me from the firft moment I beheld thee, that thou wert the image
of my friend! my heart then opened itfelf to
receive thee, as his offspring.—I had a ftrange
foreboding that I was to be thy protector.—
I would then have made thee my own, but
heaven orders things for the beft, it made thee
the inftrument of this difcovery, and in its
own time and manner conducted thee to my
arms.—praife be to God for his wonderful do-
ings towards the children of men! every thing
that has befallen thee is by his direction, and
he will not leave his work unfinifhed, I truft
that I fhall be his inftrument to do juftice on
the guilty, and to reftore the orphan of my
friend to his rights and title. I devote myfelf

to

to this fervice, and will make it the bufinefs of my life to effect it.

Edmund gave vent to his emotions, in raptures of joy and gratitude, they fpent feveral hours in this way without thinking of the time that paffed, the one enquiring, the other explaining and repeating every particular of the interefting ftory.

At length they were interrupted by the careful John Wyatt, who was anxious to know if any thing was likely to give trouble to his mafter.—fir, faid John, it grows dark, do you not want a light?—we want no light but what heaven gives us, faid fir Philip, I knew not whether it was dark or light.—I hope, faid John, nothing has happened, I hope your honour has heard no bad tidings.—I—I—I hope no offence.—none at all, faid the good knight, I am obliged to your folicitude for me; I have heard fome things that grieve me, and others that give me great pleafure, but the forrows are paft and the joys remain.—thank God! faid John, I was afraid fomething was the matter to give your honour trouble.—I thank you my good fervant! you fee this young gentleman, I would have you John, devote yourfelf to his fervice, I give you to him for an attendant on his perfon, and would have you fhow your affection to me by your attachment to him.—oh fir, faid John in a melancholy voice, what have I done to be turned out of your fervice?—no fuch matter John, faid fir Philip, you will not leave my fervice.—fir, faid John, I would rather die than leave you. —and my lad, I like you too well to part with you, but in ferving my friend you will ferve

me;

me ; know that this young man is my fon.—
your fon fir, faid John!—not my natural fon,
but my relation, my fon by adoption, my
heir !—and will he live with you fir?——yes
John, and I hope to die with him.—oh then
I will ferve him with all my heart and foul,
and I will do my beft to pleafe you both.—I
thank you John, and I will not forget your
honeft love and duty ; I have fo good an opinion of you, that I will tell you fome things
concerning this gentleman that will entitle
him to your refpect.—'tis enough for me, faid
John, to know that your honour refpects him,
to make me pay him as much duty as yourfelf.—but John, when you know him better,
you will refpect him ftill more, at prefent I
fhall only tell you what he is not, for you
think him only the fon of Andrew Twyford,
and is he not ? faid John.—no, but his wife
nurfed him, and he paffed for her fon.—and
does old Twyford know it fir?—he does, and
will bear witnefs to it ; but he is the fon of a
near friend of mine, of quality fuperior to my
own, and as fuch you muft ferve and refpect
him.—I fhall to be fure fir, but what name
fhall I call him?—you fhall know that hereafter, in the mean time bring a light and wait
on us to the other parlour.

When John was withdrawn, fir Philip faid
that is a point to be confidered and determined
immediately ; it is proper that you fhould affume a name till you can take that of your
father, for I choofe you fhould drop that of
your fofter father, and I would have you be
called by one that is refpectable.—in that and
every other point I will be wholly governed
by

by you fir, faid Edmund.—well then I will give you the name of Seagrave, I fhall fay that you are a relation of my own, and my mother was really of that family.

John foon returned and attended them into the other parlour, fir Philip entered with Edmund in his hand.—my friends, faid he, this gentlemen is mr. Edmund Seagrave, the fon of a dear friend and relation of mine, he was loft in his infancy, brought up by a good woman out of pure humanity, and is but lately reftored to his own family ; the circumftances fhall be made known hereafter, in the mean time I have taken him under my care and protection, and will ufe all my power and intereft to fee him reftored to his fortune, which is enjoyed by the ufurper who was the caufe of his expulfion, and the death of his parents ; receive him as my relation and friend ; Zadifky do you embrace him firft ! Edmund, you and this gentleman muft love each other for my fake, hereafter you will do it for your own.—they all rofe, each embraced and congratulated the young man.—Zadifky faid, fir whatever griefs and misfortunes you may have endured, you may reckon them at an end, from the hour you are beloved and protected by fir Philip Harclay. —I firmly believe it fir, replied Edmund, and my heart enjoys already more happinefs than I ever yet felt, and promifes me all that I can wifh in future, his friendfhip is the earneft heaven gives me of its bleffings hereafter.

They fat down to fupper with mutual cheartulnefs, and Edmund enjoyed the repaft with more fatisfaction than he had felt a long time,—fir Philip faw his countenance brighten

up

up, and looked on him with heart-felt pleafure.—every time I look on you, faid he, reminds me of your father, you are the fame perfon I loved twenty-three years ago; I rejoice to fee you under my roof, go to your repofe early, and to morrow we will confult farther.—Edmund withdrew, and enjoyed a night of fweet undifturbed repofe.

The next morning Edmund arofe in perfect health and fpirits; he waited on his benefactor, they were foon after joined by mr. Zadifky, who fhowed great attention and refpect to the youth, and offered him his beft fervices without referve.—Edmund accepted them with equal refpect and modefty, and finding himfelf at eafe, began to difplay his amiable qualities.—they breakfafted together, afterward fir Philip defired Edmund to walk out with him.

As foon as they were out of hearing, fir Philip faid.—I could not fleep laft night for thinking of your affairs.—I laid fchemes for you, and rejected them again, we muft lay our plan before we begin to act; what fhall be done with this treacherous kinfman?—— unhuman monfter!—this affaffin of his neareft relation!—I will rifk my life and fortune to bring him to juftice.—fhall I go to court and demand juftice of the king?—or fhall I accufe him of the murther and make him ftand a publick trial?—if I treat him as a baron of the realm he muft be tried by his peers, if as a commoner he muft be tried at the county affize; but we muft fhow reafon why he fhould be degraded from his title.—have you any thing to propofe?—nothing fir, I have only to
wifh

wifh that it might be as private as poſſible, for.
the ſake of my noble benefactor, the lord Fitz-
Owen, upon whom ſome part of the family diſgrace would naturally fall, and that would be an
ill return for all his kindneſs and generoſity to
me.—that is a generous and grateful conſide-
ration on your part, but you owe ſtill more to
the memory of your injured parents.——
however there is yet another way that ſuits
me better than any hitherto propoſed, I will
challenge the traitor to meet me in the field,
and if he has ſpirit enough to anſwer my call, I
will there bring him to juſtice, if not I will
bring him to a publick trial.

No ſir, ſaid Edmund, that is my province;
ſhould I ſtand by and ſee my noble gallant
friend expoſe his life for me, I ſhould be unworthy to bear the name of that friend whom
you ſo much lament.—it will become his ſon
to vindicate his name and revenge his death.
—I will be the challenger and no other.—and
do you think he will anſwer the challenge of
an unknown youth, with nothing but his pre-
tentions to his name and title ?—certainly not.
—leave this matter to me, I think of a way
that will oblige him to meet me at the houſe
of a third perſon who is known to all the parties concerned, and where we will have au-
thentick witneſſes of all that paſſes between
him and me ; I will deviſe the time, place
and manner, and ſatisfy all your ſcruples.—Edmund offered to reply, but ſir Philip bad him
be ſilent, and let him proceed in his own way.

He then led him over his eſtate and ſhowed
him every thing deſerving his notice, he told
him all the particulars of his domeſtick œco-

L   nomy,

nomy, and they returned home in time to meet their friends at dinner.

They spent several days in consulting how to bring sir Walter to account, and improving their friendship and confidence in each other, and Edmund endeared himself so much to his friend and patron, that he declared him his adopted son and heir before all his friends and servants, and ordered them to respect him as such.—he every day improved their love and regard for him, and be became the darling of the whole family.

After much consideration, sir Philip fixed his resolution and began to execute his purposes.—he set out for the seat of the lord Clifford, attended by Edmund, M. Zadisky, and two servants.—lord Clifford received them with kindness and hospitality.

Sir Philip presented Edmund to lord Clifford and his family, as his near relation and presumptive heir ; they spent the evening in the pleasures of convivial mirth and hospitable entertainment : the next day sir Philip began to open his mind to lord Clifford, telling him that both his young friend and himself had received great injuries from the present lord Lovel, which they were resolved to call him to account for, but that for many reasons they were desirous to have proper witnesses of all that should pass between them, begging the favour of his lordship to be the principal one.—lord Clifford acknowledged the confidence placed in him, and besought sir Philip to let him be the arbitrator between them.—sir Philip assured him that their wrongs would not admit of arbitration, as he should judge hereafter, but

that

that he was unwilling to explain them further till he knew certainly whether or not the lord Lovel would meet him, for if he refused, he must take another method with him.

Lord Clifford was defirous to know the grounds of the quarrel, but fir Philip declined entering into particulars at prefent, affuring him of a full information hereafter.—he then fent M. Zadifky, attended by John Wyatt, and a fervant of lord Clifford, with a written letter to lord Lovel, the contents were as follows.

"My lord Lovel!

"Sir Philip Harclay earneftly defires to fee
"you at the houfe of lord Clifford, where he
"waits to call you to account for the injuries
"done by you to the late Arthur lord Lovel,
"your kiniman; if you accept his demand,
"he will make the lord Clifford a witnefs and
"a judge of the caufe, if not, he will expofe
"you publickly as a traitor and a coward.—
"pleafe to anfwer this letter, and he will ac-
"quaint you with the time, place and man-
"ner of the meeting.   Philip Harclay."

Zadifky prefented the letter to lord Lovel, informing him that he was the friend of fir Philip Harclay.—he feemed furprized and confounded at the contents, but putting on an haughty air.—I know nothing, faid he, of the bufinefs this letter brings, but wait a few hours and I will give you an anfwer.—he gave orders to treat Zadifky as a gentlemen in every refpect, but in avoiding his company.—for the Greek had a fhrewd and penetrating afpect, and he obferved every turn of his countenance;

the next day he came and apologized for his
abfence, and gave him the anfwer, fending
his refpects to the lord Clifford.—the meffengers returned with all fpeed, and fir Philip read
the anfwer before all prefent.

"Lord Lovel knows not of any injuries done
"by him to the late Arthur lord Lovel, whom he
"fucceeded by juft right of inheritance; nor of
"any right fir Philip Harclay has, to call'to
"account a man to whom he is barely known,
"having feen him only once, many years
"ago, at the houfe of his uncle, the old lord
"Lovel; neverthelefs, lord Lovel will not
"fuffer any man to call his name and honour
"into queftion with impunity, for which rea-
"fon he will meet fir Philip Harclay at any
"time, place and manner he fhall appoint,
"and bringing the fame number of friends
"and dependants, that juftice may be done to
"all parties.   Lovel."

'Tis well, faid fir Philip, I am glad to find
he has the fpirit to meet me, he is an enemy
worthy of my fword.—lord Clifford then propofed, that both parties fhould pafs the borders
and obtain leave of the warden of the fcottifh
marches to decide the quarrel in his jurifdiction,
with a felect number of friends on both fides.
—fir Philip agreed to the propofal, and lord
Clifford wrote in his own name to afk permiffion of the lord Graham, that his friends might
come there, and obtained it on condition that
neither party fhould exceed a limited number
of friends and followers.

Lord Clifford fent chofen meffengers to lord
Lovel, acquainting him with the conditions,
and

and appointing the time, place and manner of
their meeting, and that he had been defired
to accept the office of judge of the field.———
lord Lovel accepted the conditions, and promifed to be their without fail.—lord Clifford
notified the fame to lord Graham, warden of
the marches, who caufed a piece of ground to
be enclofed for the lifts, and made preparations
againft the dayappointed.

In the interim fir Philip Harclay thought
proper to fettle his worldly affairs; he made
Zadifky acquainted with every circumftance
of Edmund's hiftory, and the obligation that
lay upon him to revenge the death of his
friend, and fee juftice done to his heir.———
Zadifky entered into the caufe with an ardor
that fpoke the affection he bore to his friend.
—why, faid he, would you not fuffer me to
engage this traitor?—your life is of too much
confequence to be ftaked againft his, but tho'
I truft that the juftice of your caufe muft fuc-
ceed, yet if it fhould happen otherwife, I vow
to revenge you, he fhall never go back from
us both; but my hope and truft is to fee your
arm the minifter of juftice:—fir Philip then
fent for a lawyer and made his will, by which
he appointed Edmund his chief heir by the
name of Lovel, alias Seagrave, alias Twyford;
he ordered that all his old friends, foldiers and
fervants, fhould be maintained in the fame
manner during their lives; he left to Zadifky
an annuity of an hundred a year, and a legacy
of two hundred pounds; one hundred pounds
to a certain monaftry; the fame fum to be di-
ftributed among difbanded foldiers, and the

L 3   fame

fame to the poor and needy in his neighbourhood.

.. He appointed lord Clifford joint executor
with Edmund, and gave his will into that nobleman's care, recommending Edmund to his
favour and protection.—if I live, faid he, I will
make him appear to be worthy of it, if I die he
will want a friend.—I am defirous your lordfhip,
as a judge of the field, fhould be unprejudiced
on either fide, that you may judge impartially;
if I die, Edmund's pretenfions die with me,
but my friend Zadifky will acquaint you with
the foundation of them.—I take thefe precautions becaufe I ought to be prepared for every
thing, but my heart is warm with better
hopes, and I hope to live to juftify my own
caufe, as well as that of my friend, who is a
perfon of more confequence than he appears
to be.—lord Clifford accepted the truft, and
expreffed the greateft reliance upon fir Philip's
honour and veracity.

While thefe preparations were making for
the great event that was to decide the pretenfions of Edmund, his enemies at the caftle
of Lovel were brought to fhame for their behaviour to him.

The difagreement between Wenlock and
Markham had by degrees brought on an explanation of fome parts of their conduct.—
father Ofwald had often hinted to the baron
the envy of Wenlock's behaviour to Edmund's
fuperior qualities, and the artifices by which
he had obtained fuch an influence with fir
Robert, as to make him take his part upon
all occafions.—Ofwald now took advantage of
the breach between thefe two incendiaries,

to

to perfuade Markbam to juftify himfelf at Wenlock's expence, and to tell all he knew of his wickednefs; at length he promifed to declare all he knew of Wenlock's conduct, as well in France as fince their return, when he fhould be called upon; by him Ofwald was enabled to unravel the whole of his contrivances, againft the honour, intereft, and even life of Edmund.

He prevailed on Hewfon and Kemp to add their teftimony to the others, Hewfon confeffed that he was touched in his confcience, when he reflected on the cruelty and injuftice of his behaviour to Edmund, whofe behaviour towards him, after he had laid a fnare for his life, was fo noble and generous, that he was cut to the heart by it, and had fuffered fo much pain and remorfe, that he longed for nothing fo much as an opportunity to unburden his mind; but the dread of mr. Wenlock's anger, and the effects of his refentment had hitherto kept them filent, always hoping there would come a time when he might have leave to declare the whole truth.

Ofwald conveyed this information to the baron's ear, who waited for an opportunity to make the proper ufe of it; not long after the two principal incendiaries came to an open rupture, and Markbam threatened Wenlock that he would fhow his uncle what a ferpent he had harboured in his bofom.—the baron arrefted his words, and infifting upon his telling all he knew, adding, if you fpeak the truth I will fupport you, but if you prove falfe, I will punifh you feverely; as to mr. Wenlock he fhall have a fair trial, and if all the
accufa-

accufa ons have heard are made good, it is high t me hat I fhould put him out of my family.—the baron with a fern a.pect bade them follow him into he great hall, and fent for all the reft of the tamily toge her.

He then with great folemni y old them he was ready to hear all fides of the queition.— he declared the whole fubftance of his informations, and called upon the accufers to fupport the charge.— Hewfon and Kemp gave the fame account they had done to Ofwald, offering to fwear to the truth of their teftimony; feveral of the other fervants related fuch circumftances as had come to their knowledge. —Markham then fpoke of every thing, and gave a particular account of all that had paffed on the night they fpent in the eaft apartment, he accufed himfelf of being privy to Wenlock's villany, called himfelf fool and blockhead for being the inftrument of his malignant difpofition, and afked pardon of his uncle for concealing it fo long.

The baron called upon Wenlock to reply to the charge, he inftead of anfwering, flew into a paffion, raged, fwore, threatened, and finally denied every thing.—the witneffes perfifted in their affertions.—Markham defired leave to make known the reafon they were all afraid of him, he gives it out, (faid he) that he is to be my lord's fon-in-law, and they fuppofing him to ftand firft in his favour, are afraid of his difpleafure.—I hope, faid the baron, I fhall not be at fuch a lofs for a fon-in-law, as to make choice of fuch a one as him; he never but once hinted at fuch a thing, and then I gave him no encouragement; I have long feen
there

there was fomething very wrong in him, but I did not believe he was of fo wicked a difpofition; it is no wonder that princes fhould be fo frequently deceived, when I, a private man could be fo much impofed upon within the circle of my own family; what think you fon Robert?—I fir, have been much more impofed on, and I take fhame to myfelf on the occafion.—enough, my fon, faid the baron, a generous confeffion is only a proof of growing wifdom, you are now fenfible that the beft of us are liable to impofition; the artifices of this unworthy kinfman have fet us at variance with each other, and driven away an excellent youth from this houfe, to go I know not whither; but he fhall no longer triumph in his wickednefs, he fhall feel what it is to be banifhed from the houfe of his protector, he fhall fet out for his mother's this very day, I will write to her in fuch a manner as fhall inform her that he has offended me, without particularifing the nature of his faults; I will give him an opportunity of recovering his credit with his own family, and this fhall be my fecurity againft his doing further mifchief, may he repent and be forgiven!

Markham deferves punifhment, but not in the fame degree.—I confefs it, faid he, and will fubmit to whatever your lordfhip fhall enjoin.—you fhall be only banifhed for a time, but he for ever; I will fend you abroad on a bufinefs that fhall put you in a way to do credit to yourfelf and fervice to me.—fon Robert, have you any objection to my fentence?——my lord, faid he, I have great reafon to diftruft myfelf, I am fenfible of my own weak-
nefs

nefs, and your fuperiour wifdom, as well as goodnefs, and I will henceforward fubmit to you in all things.

The baron ordered two of his fervants to pack up Wenlock's clothes and neceffaries, and to fet out with him that very day, he bad fome others keep an eye upon him left he fhould efcape; as foon as they were ready, my lord wifhed him a good journey, and gave him a letter for his mother.—he departed without faying a word, in a fullen kind of refentment, but his countenance fhowed the inward agitations of his mind.

As foon as he was gone every mouth was opened againft him, a thoufand ftories came out that they never heard before; the baron and his fons were aftonifhed that he fhould go on fo long without detection.—my lord fighed deeply at the thoughts of Edmund's expulfion, and ardently wifhed to know what was become of him.

Sir Robert took the opportunity of coming to a explanation with his brother William, he took fhame to himfelf for fome part of his paft behaviour.—mr. William owned his affection to Edmund, and juftified it by his merit and attachment to him, which were fuch that he was certain no time or diftance could alter them.—he accepted his brother's acknowledgement as a full amends for all that had paft, and begged that henceforward an entire love and confidence might ever fubfift between them.— thefe new regulations reftored peace, confidence and harmony in the caftle of Lovel.

At length the day arrived for the combatants to meet, the lord Graham with twelve followers,

lowers gentlemen, and twelve fervants were ready at the dawn of day to receive them.

The firit that entered the field was fir Philip Harclay, knight, armed compleatly, excepting his head piece, Hugh Rugby, his efquire, bearing his lance, John Barnard, his page, carrying his helmet and fpurs, two fervants in his proper livery; the next came Edmund, the heir of Lovel, followed by his fervant John Wyatt; Zadifky followed by his fervant.

At a fhort diftance came the lord Clifford, as judge of the field, with his efquire, two pages, and two livery fervants; followed by his eldeft fon, his nephew, a gentleman his friend, each attended by one fervant; he alfo brought a furgeon of note to take care of the wounded.

The lord Graham faluted them, and by his order they took their places without the lifts, and the trumpet founded for the challenger. —it was anfwered by the defendant, who foon after appeared, attended by three gentlemen his friends, with each one fervant, befide his own proper attendants.

A place was erected for the lord Clifford, as judge of the field, he defired lord Graham wou'd fhare the office, he accepted it on condition that the combatants fhould make no objection, and they agreed to it with the greateft ccurtefy and refpect; they confulted together on many points of honour and ceremony between the two combatants.

They appointed a marfhal of the field, and other inferior officers ufually employed on thefe occafions. The lord Graham fent the marfhal for the challenger, defiring him to declare

clare the caufe of his quarrel before his enemy.
—fir Philip Harclay then advanced, and thus
ipoke.

"I Philip Harclay, knight, challenge Wal-
"ter, commonly called lord Lovel, as a bafe,
"treacherous and bloody man, who by his
"wicked arts and devices, did kill, or caufe
"to be killed, his kinfman, Arthur lord
"Lovel, my dear and noble friend.—I am
"called upon in an extraordinary manner to
"revenge his death, and I will prove the truth
"of what I have affirmed at the peril of my
"life."

Lord Graham then bade the defendant anfwer to the charge.—lord Lovel ftood forth
before his followers, and thus replied.

"I Walter, baron of Lovel, do deny the
"charge againft me, and affirm it to be a bafe,
"falfe and malicious accufation of this fir
"Philip Harclay, which I believe to be in-
"vented by himfelf, or elfe framed by fome
"enemy, and told to him for wicked ends ;
"but be that as it may, I will maintain my
"own honour, and prove him to be a falfe
"traitor at the hazard of my own life, and to
"the punifhment of his prefumption."

Then faid the lord Graham, will not this
quarrel admit of arbitration?—no, replied fir
Philip, when I have juftified this charge, I
have more to bring againft him, I truft in God
and the juftice of my caufe, and defy that
traitor to the death !—lord Clifford then fpoke
a few words to lord Graham. who immediately
called to the marfhal and bad him open the
lifts, and deliver their weapons to the combatants.

While

While the marſhal was arranging the combatants, and their followers, Edmund approached his friend and patron, he put one knee to the ground, he embraced his knees with the ſtrongeſt emotions of grief and anxiety; he was dreſſed in compleat armour with his viſor down, his device was a hawthorn, with a graft of the roſe upon it, the motto—*This is not my true parent.*—but ſir Philip bad him take theſe words.-*e fruᵭu arbor cognoſcitur.*

Sir Philip embraced the youth with ſtrong marks of affeᵭion.—be compoſed my child, I have neither guilt, fear, nor doubt in me, I am ſo certain of ſucceſs that I bid you be prepared for the conſequence.—Zadiſky embraced his friend, he comforted Edmund, he ſuggeſted every thing that could confirm his hopes of ſucceſs.

The marſhal waited to deliver the ſpear to ſir Philip, he now preſented it with the uſual form.—ſir, receive your lance, and God defend the right!—ſir Philip anſwered amen! in a voice that was heard by all preſent.

He next preſented his weapon to lord Lovel with the ſame ſentence, who likewiſe anſwered amen! with a good courage.—immediately the liſts were cleared, and the combatants began the fight.

They contended a long time with equal ſkill and courage, at length ſir Philip unhorſed his antagoniſt.—the judges ordered, that either he ſhould alight, or ſuffer his enemy to remount, he choſe the former, and a ſharp combat on foot enſued.—the ſweat rolled off their bodies with the violence of the exerciſe.—ſir Philip watched every motion of his enemy, and ſtrove

M   to

to weary him out, intending to wound but not to kill him, unlefs obliged for his own fafety.

He thruft his fword through his left arm, and demanded whether he would confefs the fact.—lord Lovel enraged, anfwered, he would die fooner.—fir Philip then paffed the fword through his body twice, and lord Lovel fell, crying out that he was flain.

I hope not, faid fir Philip, for I have a great deal of bufinefs for you to do before you die; confefs your fins and endeavour to attone for them, as the only ground to hope for pardon. —lord Lovel faid, you are the victor, ufe your good fortune generoufly!

Sir Philip took away his fword, and then waved it over his head, and beckoned for affiftance.—the judges fent to beg fir Philip to fpare the life of his enemy.—I will, faid he, upon condition that he will make an honeft confeffion.

Lord Lovel defired a furgeon and a confeffor. —you fhall have both, faid fir Philip, but you muft firft anfwer me a queftion or two.——did you kill your kinfman or not?—it was not my hand that killed him, anfwered the wounded man.—it was done by your own order however; you fhall have no affiftance till you anfwer this point?—it was, faid he, and heaven is juft!—bear witnefs all prefent, faid fir Philip, he confeffes the fact!

He then beckoned Edmund, who approached.—take off your helmet, faid he, look on that youth, he is the fon of your injured kinfman.—it is himfelf! faid the lord Lovel, and fainted away.

Sir

Sir Philip then called for a furgeon and a prieft, both of which lord Graham had provided; the former began to bind up his wounds, and his affiftants poured a cordial into his mouth.—preferve his life if it be poffible, faid fir Philip, for much depends upon it.

He then took Edmund by the hand, and prefented him to all the company.——in this young man, faid he, you fee the true heir of the houfe of Lovel! heaven has in its own way made him the inftrument to difcover the death of his parents; his father was affafinated by order of that wicked man, who now receives his punifhment; his mother was by his cruel treatment compelled to leave her own houfe, fhe was delivered in the fields, and perifhed herfelf in feeking a fhelter for her infant; I have fufficient proofs of every thing I fay, which I am ready to communicate to every perfon who defires to know the particulars; heaven by my hand has chaftifed him, he has confeffed the fact I accufe him of, and it remains that he make reftitution of the fortune and honours he hath ufurped fo long.

Edmund kneeled, and with uplifted hands returned thanks to heaven, that his noble friend and champion was crowned with victory!—the lords and gentlemen gathered round them, they congratulated them both, while lord Lovel's friends and followers were employed in taking care of him.—lord Clifford took fir Philip's hand.—you have acted with fo much honour and prudence that it is prefumptuous to offer you advice, but what mean you to do with the wounded man?—I have not determined, faid he, I thank you for the hint,

M 2   and

and beg your advice how to proceed.—let us consult lord Graham, said he.—lord Graham insisted upon their going all to his castle, there said he, you will have impartial witnesses of all that passes.—sir Philip was unwilling to give so much trouble.—the lord Graham protested he should be proud to do any service to so noble a gentleman.—lord Clifford enforced his request, saying, it was better upon all accounts to keep their prisoner on this side the borders till they saw what turn his health would take, and to keep him safely till he had settled his worldly affairs.

This resolution being taken, lord Graham invited the wounded man and his friends to his castle, as being the nearest place where he could be lodged and taken proper care of, it being dangerous to carry him further.—they accepted the proposal with many acknowledgements, and having made a kind of litter of boughs, they all proceeded to lord Graham's castle, where they put lord Lovel to bed, and the surgeon dressed his wounds, and desired he might be kept quiet, not knowing at present whether they were dangerous or not.

About an hour after, the wounded man complained of thirst, he asked for the surgeon, and enquired if his life was in danger, the surgeon answered him, doubtfully.——he asked, where is sir Philip Harclay ?—in the castle.—where is that young man whom he calls the heir of Lovel ?—he is here too.—then I am surrounded with my enemies, I want to speak to one of my own servants, without witnesses, let one be sent to me.

The

The furgeon withdrew, and acquainted the gentlemen below.—he fhall not fpeak to any man, faid fir Philip, but in my prefence.—he went with him into the fick man's room.—upon the fight of fir Philip, he feemed in great agitation—am I not allowed to fpeak with my own fervant, faid he?—yes fir, you may, but not without witnefles.—then I am a prifoner it feems? no, not fo fir, but fome caution is necefiary at prefent, but compofe yourfeif, I do not wifh for your death,—then why did you feek it? I never injured you.—yes you have, in the perfon of my friend, and I am only the inftrument of juftice in the hand of heaven; endeavour to make atonement while life is fpared to you.—fhall I fend the prieft to you? perhaps he may convince you of the neceffity of reftitution, in order to obtain forgivenefs of your fins.

Sir Philip fent for the prieft and the furgeon, and obliged the fervant to retire with him.—I leave you fir to the care of thefe gentlemen, and whenever a third perfon is admitted, I will be his attendant, I will vifit you again within an hour.—he then retired, and confulted his friends below; they were of an opinion that no time fhould be loft.—you will then, faid he, accompany me into the fick man's apartment in an hour's time.

Within the hour, fir Philip, attended by lord Clifford and lord Graham entered the chamber, lord Lovel was in great emotion, the prieft ftood on one fide of the bed, the furgeon on the other, the former exhorted him to confefs his fins, the other defired he might be left to his repofe.—lord Lovel feemed in great

M 3   anguifh

anguifh of mind, he trembled, and was in the utmoft confufion.—fir Philip intreated him with the piety of a confeffor, to confider his foul's health before that of his body; he then afked fir Philip, by what means he knew that he was concerned in the death of his kinf-man?—fir, faid he, it was not merely by hu-man means this fact was difcovered.—there is a certain apartment in the caftle of Lovel, that has been fhut up thefe one and twenty years, but has lately been opened and examined into.

Oh heaven! exclaimed he, then Geoffrey muft have betrayed me!—no fir he has not, it was revealed in a very extraordinary man-ner to that youth whom it moft concerns.— how can he be the heir of Lovel?—by being the fon of that unfortunate woman, whom you cruelly obliged to leave her own houfe, to avoid being compelled to wed the murderer of her hufband; moreover we are not igno-rant of the fictious funeral you made for her. —all is difcovered, and you will not tell us any more than we know already.—but we de-fire to have it confirmed by your confeffion.— the judgments of heaven are fallen upon me! faid lord Lovel.—I am childlefs, and one is arifen from the grave to claim my inheritance. —nothing then hinders you to do juftice and make reftitution, it is for the eafe of your confcience, and you have no other way of making atonement for all the mifchief you have done.—you know too much, faid the criminal, and I will relate what you do not know.

You

You may remember that I faw you once at my uncle's houfe?—I well remember it.—— at that time my mind was difturbed by the baleful paffion of envy, it was from that root all my bad actions fprung.—praife be to God! faid the good prieft, he hath touched your heart with true contrition, and you fhow the effect of his mercies, you will do juftice, and you will be rewarded by the gift of repentance unto falvation.—fir Philip defired the penitent to proceed.

My kinfman excelled me in every kind of merit, in the graces of perfon and mind, in all his exercifes, and in every accomplifhment.—I was totally eclipfed by him, and I hated to be in his company, but what finifhed my averfion was his addreffing the lady upon whom I had fixed my affections; I ftrove to rival him there, but fhe gave him the preference, that indeed was only his due, but I could not bear to fee or acknowledge it.

The moft bitter hatred took poffeffion of my breaft, and I vowed to revenge the fuppofed injury as foon as opportunity fhould offer; I buried my refentment deep in my heart, and outwardly appeared to rejoice at his fuccefs; I made a merit of refigning my pretenfions to him, but I could not bear to be prefent at his nuptials: I retired to my father's feat, and brooded over my revenge in fecret. —my father died this year, and foon after my uncle followed him; within another year my kinfman was fummoned to attend the king on his Welch expedition.

As foon as I heard he was gone from home I refolved to prevent his return, exulting in
the

the profpect of poffeffing his title, fortune and
his lady; I hired meffengers who were con-
ftantly going and coming to give me intelligence ot all that paffed at the caftle; I went
foon after under pretence of vifiting my kinfman, my fpies brought me an account of all
that happened; one informed me of the event
of the battle, but could not tell whether my
rival was living or dead, I hoped the latter,
that I might avoid the crime I meditated; I
reported his death to his lady, who took it very
heavily.

Soon after a meffenger arrived with tidings
that he was alive and well, and had obtained
leave to return home immediately.

I inftantly difpatched my two emiffaries to
intercept him on the way; he made fo much
hafte to return, that he was met within a mile
of his own caftle, he had out rode his fervants
and was alone, they killed him and drew him
afide out of the highway; they then came to
me with all fpeed, and defired my orders, it
was then about funfet; I fent them back to
fetch the dead body, which they brought privately into the caftle; they ties it neck and
heels and put it into a trunk, which they buried under the floor in the clofet you mentioned; the fight of the body ftung me to the
heart, I then felt the pangs of remorfe, but it
was too late; I took every precaution that
prudence fuggefted to prevent the difcovery,
but nothing can be concealed from the eye of
heaven.

From that fatal hour I have never known
peace, always in fear of fomething impending
to difcover my guilt, and to bring me to
                                          fhame;

ſhame; at length I am overtaken by juſtice, I
am brought to a ſevere reckoning here, and
I dread to meet one more ſevere hereafter.

Enough, ſaid the prieſt, you have done a
good work my ſon! truſt in the Lord, and
now this burden is off your mind, the reſt will
be made eaſy to you.

Lord Lovel took a minute's repoſe, and
then went on.—I hope by the hint you gave,
ſir Philip, the poor lady is yet alive?—no ſir,
ſhe is not, but ſhe died not till after ſhe brought
forth a ſon, whom heaven made its inſtrument to diſcover and avenge the death of
both his parents.—they are well avenged, ſaid
he, I have no children to lament for me, all
mine have been taken from me in the bloom
of youth, only one lived to be twelve years
old; I intended her for a wife for one of my
nephews, but within three months I have buried her.—he ſighed, wept, and was ſilent.

The gentlemen preſent lifted up their hands
and eyes to heaven in ſilence.—the will of
heaven be obeyed, ſaid the prieſt!—my penitent hath confeſſed all, what more would you
require?—that he make atonement, ſaid ſir
Philip, that he ſurrender the title and eſtate to
the right heir, and diſpoſe of his own proper
fortune to his neareſt relations, and reſign himſelf to penitence and preparation for a future
ſtate; for this time I leave him with you father, and will join my prayers for his repentance.

So ſaying, he left the room and was followed by the barons and the ſurgeon, and the
prieſt remained alone with him; as ſoon as
they were out of hearing, ſir Philip queſtioned
the

the furgeon concerning his patient's fituation, he anfwered that at prefent he faw no figns of immediate danger, but he could not yet pronounce that there was none; if he were mortally wonnded he could not be fo well, nor fpeak fo long without faintnefs, and it is my opinion, faid he, that he will foon recover, if nothing happens to retard the cure.—then faid fir Philip, keep this opinion from him, for I would fuffer the fear of death to operate on him, until he hath performed fome neceffary acts of juftice, let it only be known to thefe noblemen, upon whofe honour I can rely, and I truft they will approve my requeft to you fir. —I join in it, faid lord Clifford, from the fame motives—I infift upon it, faid lord Graham, and I can anfwer for my furgeon's difcretion. —my lords, faid the furgeon, you may depend on my fidelity, and after what I have juft heard, my confcience is engaged in this noble gentleman's behalf, and I will do every thing in my power to fecond your intentions.——I thank you fir, faid fir Philip, and you may depend on my gratitude in return; I prefume you will fit up with him to night, if any danger fhould arife, I defire to be called immediately, but otherwife I would fuffer him to reft quietly, that he may be prepared for the bufinefs of the following day.—I fhall obey your directions fir, and my neceffary attendance will give me a pretence not to leave him, and thus I fhall hear all that paffes between him and all that vifit him.—you will oblige me highly, faid fir Philip, and I fhall go to reft with confidence in your care.

The

The furgeon returned to the tick man's chamber, fir Philip and the barons to the company below; they fupped in the great hall with all the gentlemen that were prefent at the combat.—fir Philip and his Edmund retired to their repofe, being heartily fatigued, and the company ftaid to a late hour, commenting upon the action of the day, praifing the courage and generofity of the noble knight, and wifhing a good event to his undertaking.

Moft of lord Lovel's friends went away as foon as they faw him fafely lodged, being afhamed of him, and of their appearance in his behalf, and the few that ftayed were induced by their defire of a further information of the bafe action he had committed, and to juftify their own characters and conduct.

The next morning fir Philip entered into confultation with the two barons, on the methods he fhould take to get Edmund received, and acknowledged as heir of the houfe of Lovel.—they were all of opinion that the criminal fhould be kept in fear till he had fettled his worldly affairs, and they had refolved how to difpofe of him.—with this determination they entered his room, and enquired of the furgeon how he had paffed the night, he fhook his head, and faid but little.

Lord Lovel defired that he might be removed to his own houfe.—lord Graham faid he could not confent to that, as there was evident danger in removing him, and appealed to the furgeon who confirmed his opinion.—lord Graham defired he would make himfelf eafy, and that he fhould have every kind of affiftance there.

Sir

Sir Philip then propofed to fend for the lord Fitz-Owen, who would fee that all poffible care was taken of his brother-in-law, and would affift him in fettling his affairs.—lord Lovel was againft it, he was peevifh and un- eafy, and defired to be left with only his own fervants to attend him.—fir Philip left the room with a fignificant look, and the two lords endeavoured to reconcile him to his fitu- ation.—he interrupted them.—it is eafy for men in your fituation to advife, but it is diffi- cult for one in mine to practice, wounded in body and mind, it is natural that I fhould ftrive to avoid the extremes of fhame and punifh- ment ; I thank you for your kind offices, and beg I may be left with my own fervants.—— with them and the furgeon you fhall, faid lord Graham, and they both retired.

Sir Philip met them below.—my lords, faid he, I am defirous that my lord Fitz-Owen fhould be fent for, and that he may hear his brother's confeffion, for I fufpect that he may hereafter deny, what only the fear of death has extorted from him ; with your permiffion I am determined to fend meffengers to day.— they both expreffed approbation, and lord Clifford propofed to write to him, faying, a letter from an impartial perfon will have the more weight ; I will fend one of my principal domefticks with your own.—this meafure be- ing refolved upon, lord Clifford retired to write, and fir Philip to prepare his fervants for inftant departure.—Edmund defired leave to write to father Ofwald, and John Wyatt was ordered to be the bearer of his letter.—when the lord Clifford had finifhed his letter, he read

it

it to fir Philip, and his chofen friends as follows.

" Right Hon. my good Lord,

" I have taken upon me to acquaint your
" lordfhip, that there has been a folemn com-
" bat at arms between your brother-in-law,
" the lord Lovel, and fir Philip Harclay, knt.
" of Yorkfhire.—it was fought in the jurif-
" diction of the lord Graham, who with my-
" felf was appointed judge of the field, it
" was fairly won, and fir Philip is the con-
" queror.—after he had gained the victory he
" declared at large the caufe of the quarrel,
" and that he had revenged the death of Ar-
" thur lord Lovel his friend, whom the prefent
" lord Lovel had affaffinated, that he might
" enjoy his title and eftate.—the wounded
" man confeffed the fact, and fir Philip gave
" him his life, and only carried off his fword
" as a trophy of his victory.—both the vic-
" tor and the vanquifhed were conveyed to
" lord Graham's caftle, where the lord Lovel
" now lies in great danger.—he is defirous to
" fettle his worldly affairs, and to make his
" peace with God and man.—fir Philip Har-
" clay fays, there is a male heir of the houfe
" of Lovel, for whom he claims the title and
" eftate; but he is very defirous that your
" lordfhip fhould be prefent at the difpofal
" of your brother's property, that of right be-
" longs to him, of which your children are
" the undoubted heirs.—he alfo wants to con-
" fult you in many other points of honour and
" equity.—let me intreat you on the receipt
" of this letter, to fet out immediately for

" lord

" lord Graham's caftle, where you will be re-
" ceived with the utmoft refpect and hofpita-
" lity.—you will hear things that will fur-
" prize.you as much as they do me.—you will
" judge of them with that juftice and honour
" that fpeaks your character, and you will
" unite with us in wondering at the ways of
" providence, and fubmitting to its decrees.—
" in punifhing the guilty, and doing juftice to
" the innocent and oppreffed.—my beft wifhes
" and prayers attend you and your hopeful fami-
" ly.—my lord I remain your humble fervant.
" Clifford."

Every one prefent exprefled the higheft approbation of this letter.—fir Philip gave orders
to John Wyatt to be very circumfpect in his
behaviour, to give Edmund's letter privately
to father Ofwald, and to make no mention of
him, or his pretenfions at Lovel caftle.

Lord Clifford gave his fervant the requifite
precautions.—lord Graham added a note of invitation, and fent it by a fervant of his own.—
as foon as all things were ready, the meffengers fet out with all fpeed for the caftle of
Lovel.

They ftaid no longer by the way than to
take fome refrefhment, but rode night and
day till they arrived there.

Lord Fitz-Owen was in the parlour with his
children, father Ofwald was walking in the
avenue before the houfe, when he faw three
meffengers whofe horfes feemed jaded and the
riders fatigued, like men come a long journey.
—he came up juft as the firft had delivered his
meffage to the porter.—John Wyatt knew
him,

him, he difmounted, and made figns that he
had fomething to fay to him, he retired back
a few fteps, and John, with great dexterity,
flipped a letter into his hand.—the father gave
him his blefling and a welcome.—who do you
come from, faid he aloud ?—from the lords
Graham and Clifford to the lord FitzOwen, and
we bring letters of confequence to the baron.

Ofwald followed the meffengers into the
hall, a fervant announced their arrival.—lord
Fitz-Owen received them in the parlour, lord
Clifford's fervant delivered his mafter's letter,
lord Graham's his, and they faid they would
retire and wait his lordfhip's anfwer.—the baron ordered them fome refrefhment.—they retired, and he opened his letters; he read them
with great agitations, he ftruck his hand upon
his heart, he exclaimed.—my fears are all ve-
refied! the blow is ftruck, and it has fallen
upon the guilty !

Ofwald came in a minute after.——you are
come in good time, faid the baron, read that
letter, that my children may know the contents.—he read it with faltering voice and
trembling limbs.—they were all in great furprize.—William looked down and kept a ftu-
died filence.—fir Robert exclaimed, is it poffible ? can my uncle be guilty of fuch an action ?—you hear, faid the baron, he has con-
fefled it !—but to whom ? faid fir Robert.—his
father replied, lord Clifford's honour is unquef-
tionable, and I cannot doubt what he affirms.

Sir Robert leaned his head upon his hand
and feemed loft in thought.——at length he
feemed to awake.—my lord, I have no doubt
that Edmund is at the bottom of this bufinefs;

do you not remember that sir Philip Harclay long ago promised him his friendship; Edmund disappears, and soon after this man challenges my uncle; you know what passed here before his departure; he has suggested this affair to sir Philip, and instigated him to this action; this is the return he has made for the favours he has received from our family, to which he owes every thing.—Softly my son! said the baron, let us be cautious of reflecting upon Edmund, there is a greater hand in this business, my conjecture was too true; it was in that fatal apartment that he was made acquainted with the circumstances of lord Lovel's death, he was perhaps enjoined to reveal them to sir Philip Harclay, the bosom friend of the deceased; the mystery of that apartment is disclosed, the woe to the guilty is accomplished! there is no reflection upon any one, heaven effects its purposes in its own time and manner; I and mine are innocent, let us worship, and be silent!

But what do you propose to do, said sir Robert?—to return with the messengers, answered the baron; I think it highly proper that I should see your uncle, and hear what he has to say; my children are his heirs, in justice to them I ought to be acquainted with every thing that concerns the disposal of his fortune. —your lordship is in the right, answered sir Robert, it concerns us all; I have only to ask your permission to bear you company?—with all my heart, said the baron, I have only to ask of you in return, that you will command yourself, and not speak your mind hastily, wait for the proofs before you give judgment,

and

and take advice of your reafon before you decide upon any thing; if you reflect upon the paft, you will find reafon to diftruft yourfelf; leave all to me, and be affured I will protect your honour and my own.—I will obey you in all things my lord, and will make immediate preparation for our departure.—fo faying he left the room.

As foon as he was gone, mr. William broke filence.—my lord, if you have no great objection, I beg leave alfo to accompany you both?—you fhall my fon if you defire it; I think I can fee your motives, and your brother's alfo; your coolnefs will be a good balance to his warmth; you fhall go with us; my fon Walter fhall be his fifter's protector in our abfence, and he fhall be mafter here till we return.—I hope my dear father that will not be long, I fhall not be happy till you come home, faid the fair Emma.—it fhall be no longer my deareft, than till this untoward affair is fettled. —the baron defired to know when the meffengers were expected to return.—Ofwald took the opportunity to retire, he went to his own apartment, and read the letter, as follows.

" The heir of Lovel, to his dear and reve-
" rend friend, father Ofwald.

" Let my friends at the caftle of Lovel
" know that I live in hopes one day to fee
" them there, if you could by any means
" return with the meffengers, your teftimony
" would add weight to mine, perhaps you
" might have permiffion to attend the baron;
" I leave it to you to manage.— John Wyatt
" will inform you of all that has paffed here,

N 3   " and

" and that hitherto my fuccefs has outran my
" expectation, and almoſt my wiſhes.—I am
" in the high road to my inheritance, and
" truſt that the power who hath conducted
" me thus far, will not leave his work unfi-
" niſhed.—tell my beloved William that I
" live, and hope to embrace him before long.
" I recommend myſelf to your holy prayers
" and bleſſing, and remain your ſon and ſer-
" vant.   Edmund."

Ofwald then went to the meſſengers, he
drew John Wyatt to a diſtance from the reſt,
and got the information he wanted; he ſtayed
with him till he was ſent for to the baron.—
he went to him directly, and prevented his
queſtions.—I have been talking with the meſſengers, ſaid he, I find they have travelled
night and day to bring the letters with all
ſpeed, they only require one nights reſt, and
will be ready to ſet out with you to-morrow.
—'tis well, ſaid the baron, we will ſet out as
ſoon as they are ready.—my lord, ſaid Ofwald,
I have a favour to beg of you, it is that I may
attend you, I have ſeen the progreſs of this
wonderful diſcovery, and I have a great deſire to ſee the concluſion of it, perhaps my
preſence may be of ſervice in the courſe of
your buſineſs.—perhaps it may, ſaid the baron, I have no objection if you deſire to go.—
they then ſeparated, and went to prepare for
their journey.

Ofwald had a private interview with Joſeph,
whom he informed of all that he knew, and
his reſolution to attend the baron in his journey to the north.—I go, ſaid he, to bear witneſs

ness in behalf of injured innocence, if it be
needful I shall call upon you, therefore hold
yourself in readiness in case you should be sent
for.—that I will, said Joseph, and spend my
last remains of life and strength, to help my
young lord to his right and title ; but do they
not begin to suspect who is the heir of Lovel?
—not in the least, said Ofwald, they think him
concerned in the discovery, but have no idea
of his being interested in the event.—ch father, said Joseph, I shall think every day a
week till your return, but I will no longer
keep you from your repose.—good night, said
Oswald, but I have another visit to pay before
I go to rest.

He left Joseph and went on tip-toe to mr.
William's room and tapped at his door, he
came and opened it.—what news father?——
not much, I have only orders to tell you that
Edmund is well, and as much your friend as
ever.—I guessed, said William that we should
hear something of him.—I have still another
guess.—what is that my child?—that we shall
see or hear of him where we are a going.—
it is very likely, said Ofwald, and I would
have you be prepared for it.—I am confident
we shall hear nothing to his discredit.—I am
certain of that, said William, and I shall rejoice to see him ; I conclude that he is under
the protection of sir Philip Harclay.—he is so,
said Ofwald, I had my information from sir
Philip's servant, who is one of the messengers, and was guide to the others in their
way hither ; after some conversation they separated, and each went to his repose.

The

The next morning the whole party sat out
on their journey, they travelled by easy stages
on account of the baron's health, which began
to be impaired, and arrived in health and spirits at the castle of lord Graham, where they
were received with the utmost respect and
kindness by the noble master.

The lord Lovel had recovered his health
and strength as much as possible in the time,
and was impatient to be gone from thence to
his own house.—he was surprized to hear of
the arrival of his brother and nephews, and
expressed no pleasure at the thoughts of see-
ing them.—when sir Philip Harclay came to
pay his respects to baron Fitz-Owen, the latter received him with civility, but with a
coldness that was aparent.—sir Robert left the
room, doubting his resolution.—sir Philip came
and took the baron by the hand.—my lord I
rejoice to see you here! I cannot be satisfied
with the bare civilities of such a man as you.
—I aspire to your esteem, to your friendship,
and I shall not be happy till I obtain them;
I will make you the judge of every part of
my conduct, and where you shall condemn
me, I will condemn myself.

The baron was softened, his noble heart
felt its alliance with its counterpart, but he
thought the situation of his brother demanded
some reserve towards the man who sought his
life; but in spight of himself it wore off every
moment.—lord Clifford related all that had
passed, with the due regard to sir Philip's
honour; he remarked how nobly he concealed
the cause of his resentment against the lord
Lovel till the day of combat, that he might
                                              not

not prepossess the judges against him.—he enlarged on his humanity to the vanquished, on the desire he expressed to have justice done to his heirs ; finally, he mentioned his great respect for the lord Fitz-Owen, and the solicitude he shewed to have him come to settle the estate of the sick man in favour of his children.—lord Clifford also employed his son to soften sir Robert, and to explain to him every doubtful part of sir Philip's behaviour.

After the travellers had taken some rest, the lord Graham proposed that they should make a visit to the sick man's chamber.—the lords sent to acquaint him they were coming to visit him, and they followed the messenger.—the lord Fitz-Owen went up to the bedside, he embraced his brother with strong emotions of concern.—sir Robert followed him, then mr. William.—lord Lovel embraced them, but said nothing ; his countenance shewed his inward agitations.—lord Fitz-Owen first broke silence. —I hope I see my brother better than I expected ?—lord Lovel bit his fingers, he pulled the bed clothes, he seemed almost distracted ; at length he broke out.—I owe no thanks to those who sent for my relations ! sir Philip Harclay, you have used ungenerously the advantage you have gained over me! you spared my life only to take away my reputation, you have exposed me to strangers, and what is worse, to my dearest friends ; when I lay in a state of danger, you obliged me to say any thing, and now you take advantage of it, to ruin me in my friends affection, but if I recover, you may repent it !

Sir

Sir Phi'ip then came forward —my lords, I shall take no no'ice of what this unhappy man has jutt now faid, I fhall appeal to you, as to the honourable witneffes of all that has paffed, you fee it was no more than neceffary; I appeal to you for the motives of my treatment of him; before, at, and after our meeting; I did not take his life as I might have done, I wifhed him to repent of his fins, and to make reftitution of what he unjuftly poffeffes; I was called out to do an act of juftice; I had taken the heir of Lovel under my protection, my chief view was to fee juftice done to him, what regarded this man was but a fecondary motive; this was my end, and I will never, never lofe fight of it.

Lord Lovel feemed almoft choacked with paffion, to fee every one giving fome mark of approbation and refpect to fir Philip.——he called out, I demand to know who is this pretended heir whom he brings out to claim my title and fortune?—my noble auditors, faid fir Philip, I fhall appeal to your judgment in regard to the proofs of my wards birth and family! every circumftance fhall be laid before you, and you fhall decide upon them.

Here is a young man fuppofed the fon of a peafant, who by a train of circumftances that could not have happened by human contrivance, difcovers not only who are his real parents, but that they came to untimely deaths. —he even difcovers the different places where their bones are buried, both out of confecrated ground, and appeals to their afhes for the truth of his pretenfions.—he has alfo living proofs to offer, that will convince the moft incredulous.

lous.—I have deferred entering into particulars till the arrival of baron Fitz-Owen; I know his noble heart and honourable character, from one that has long been an eye witness of his goodness; such is the opinion I have of his justice, that I will accept him as one of the judges in his brother's cause; I and my ward will bring our proofs before him, and the company here present, in the course of them it will appear that he is the best qualified of any to judge of them, because he can ascertain many of the facts we shall have occasion to mention; I will rest our cause upon their decision.

Lord Graham applauded sir Philip's appeal, affirming his own impartiality, and calling upon lord Clifford and his son, and also his own nephews who were present.——lord Clifford said, sir Philip offers fairly, and like himself; there can be no place nor persons more impartial than the present, and I presume the lord Lovel can have no objection.—— no objection, answered he! what to be tried like a criminal, to have judges appointed over me, to decide upon my right, to my own estate and title? I will not submit to such a jurisdiction!—then, said sir Philip, you had rather be tried by the laws of the land, and have them pronounce sentence upon you?— take your choice, sir, if you refuse the one, you shall be certain of the other.—lord Clifford then said, you will allow lord Lovel to consider of the proposal, he will consult his friends, and be determined by their advice.— lord Fitz-Owen said, I am very much surprized at what I have heard, I should be glad

to

to know all that fir Philip Harclay has to fay
for his ward, that I may judge what my brother has to hope or fear; I will then give my
beft advice, or offer my mediation as he may
ftand in need of them.—you fay well, faid
lord Graham, and pray let us come directly
to the point; fir Philip you will introduce your
ward to this company, and enter upon your
proofs.

Sir Philip bowed to the company, he went
out and brought in Edmund, encouraging him
by the way; he prefented him to baron Fitz-
Owen, who looked very ferious.—Edmund
Twyford, faid he, are you the heir of the
houfe of Lovel?—I am my lord, faid Edmund,
bowing to the ground, the proofs will appear,
but I am at the fame time the moft humble
and grateful of all your fervants, and the fervant of your virtues.—fir Robert rofe up and
was going to leave the room.—fon Robert,
ftay, faid the baron, if there is any fraud you
will be pleafed to detect it, and if all that is
affirmed be true, you will not fhut your eyes
againft the light, you are concerned in this
bufinefs, hear it in filence, and let reafon be
arbiter in your caufe.—he bowed to his father, bit his lip, and retired to the window.—
William nodded to Edmund, and was filent.
—all the company had their eyes fixed on
the young man, who ftood in the midft,
cafting down his eyes with modeft refpect to
the audience; while fir Philip related all the
material circumftances of his life, the wonderful gradation by which he came to the
knowledge of his birth, the adventures of the
haunted apartment, the difcovery of the fatal
closet,

closet, and the presumptive proofs that lord Lovel was buried there.—at this place lord Fitz-Owen interrupted him.—where is this closet you talk of, for I and my sons went over the apartment since Edmund's departure, and found no such place as you describe?— my lord, said Edmund, I can account for it, the door is covered with tapestry, the same as the room, and you might easily overlook it; but I have a witness here, said he, and putting his hand into his bosom, he drew out the key. —if this is not the key of that closet, let me be deemed an impostor, and all I say a falsehood, I will risk my pretensions upon this proof.

And for what purpose did you take it away? said the baron.—to prevent any person from going into it, said Edmund, I have vowed to keep it till I shall open that closet before witnesses appointed for that purpose.—proceed sir, said the baron Fitz-Owen.—sir Philip then related the conversation between Edmund and Margery Twyford, his supposed mother.—— lord Fitz-Owen seemed in the utmost surprize, —he exclaimed, can this be true?—strange discovery!—unfortunate child!——Edmund's tears bore witness to his veracity, he was obliged to hide his face, he lifted up his clasped hands to heaven, and was in great emotions during all this part of the relation, while lord Lovel groaned, and seemed in great agitation.

Sir Philip addressed himself to lord Fitz-Owen.—my lord, there was another person present at the conversation between Edmund and his foster-mother, who can witness to all that passed; perhaps your lordship can tell

O   who

who that was ?—it was father Ofwald, replied the baron, I well remember that he went with him at his requeſt, let him be called in.—he was ſent for, and came immediately.—the baron deſired him to relate all that paſſed between Edmund and his mother.

Ofwald then began.—ſince I am now properly called upon to teſtify what I know concerning this young man, I will ſpeak the truth without fear or favour of any one, and I will ſwear by the rules of my holy order, to the truth of what I ſhall relate.—he then gave a particular account of all that paſſed on that occaſion, and mentioned the tokens found on both the infant and his mother.—where are theſe tokens to be ſeen, ſaid the lord Clifford ? —I have them here, my lord, ſaid Edmund, and I keep them as my greateſt treaſures.—— he then produced them before all the company.—there is no appearance of any fraud or colluſion, ſaid lord Graham, if any man thinks he ſees any, let him ſpeak.—pray my lord, ſuffer me to ſpeak a word, ſaid ſir Robert.— do you remember that I hinted my ſuſpicions concerning father Ofwald, the night our kinſmen lay in the eaſt apartment ?—I do, ſaid the baron.—well ſir, it now appears that he did know more than he would tell us, you find he is very deep in all Edmund's ſecrets, and you may judge what were his motives for undertaking this journey.—I obſerve what you ſay, anſwered his father, but let us hear all that Ofwald has to ſay, I will be as impartial as poſſible.—my lord, ſaid Ofwald, I beg you alſo to recollect what I ſaid on the night your ſon ſpeaks of, concerning ſecrecy in certain matters.

ters?—I remember that alfo, faid the baron, but proceed.—my lord, faid Ofwald, I knew more than I thought myfelf at liberty to dif-clofe at that time, but I will now tell you every thing.—I faw there was fomething more than common in the accidents that befel this young man, and in his being called out to fleep in the eaft apartment; I earneftly defired him to let me be with him on the fecond night, to which he confented reluctantly; we heard a great noife in the rooms underneath, we went down ftairs together, I faw him open the fatal clofet, I heard groans that pierced me to the heart, I kneeled down and prayed for the repofe of the fpirit departed, I found a feal with the arms of Lovel engraven upon it, which I gave to Edmund, and he now has it in his poffeffion; he enjoined me to keep fe-cret what I had feen and heard, till the time fhould come to declare it. I conceived that I was called to be a witnefs of thefe things, befides my curiofity was excited to know the event, I therefore defired to be prefent at the interview between him and his mother, which was affecting beyond expreffion; I heard what I have now declared as nearly as my memory permits me, I hope no impartial perfon will blame me for any part of my conduct, but if they fhould, I do not repent it, if I fhould for-feit the favour of the rich and great, I fhall have acquitted myfelf to God and my con-fcience; I have no worldly ends to anfwer, I plead the caufe of the injured orphan, and I think alfo that I fecond the defigns of providence. —you have well fpoken father, faid the lord Clifford, your witnefs is indeed of confequence.

O 2   It

It is amazing and convincing, said lord Graham, and the whole ftory is fo well connected,
that I can fee nothing to make us doubt the
truth of it; but let us examine the proofs.
—Edmund gave into their hands the necklace
and earings, he fhewed them the locket with
the cypher of Lovel, and the feal with the
arms; he told them the cloak in which he
was wrapped was in the cuftody of his fofter-
mother, who would produce it on demand.—
he begged that fome proper perfons might be
commiffioned to go with him to examine whether or no the bodies of his parents were buried where he affirmed, adding that he put
his pretenfions into their hands with pleafure,
relying entirely upon their honour and juftice.

During the interefting fcene, the criminal
covered his face and was filent, but he fent
forth bitter fighs and groans that denoted the
anguifh of his heart; at length lord Graham
in compaffion to him, propofed that they fhould
retire and confider of the proofs, adding, lord
Lovel muft needs be fatigued, we will refume
the fubject in his prefence, when he is difpofed to receive us.—fir Philip Harclay approached the bed.—fir, I now leave you in the
hands of your own relations, they are men of
ftrict honour, and I confide in them to take
care of you and of your concerns.—they then
went out of the room leaving only the lord
Fitz-Owen and his fons with the criminal.—
they difcourfed of the wonderful ftory of Edmund's birth, and the principal events of his life.

After dinner fir Philip requefted another conference with the lords, and their principal
friends.—there was prefent alfo, father Ofwald
                                             and

and lord Graham's confeſſor, who had taken
the lord Lovel's confeſſion, Edmund and Za-
dſky.—Now gentlemen, ſaid ſir Philip, I deſire to know your opinion of our proofs, and
your advice upon them.

Lord Graham ſaid, I am deſired to ſpeak
for the reſt; we think there are ſtrong pre-
ſumptive proofs that this young man is the true
heir of Lovel, but they ought to be confirmed
and authenticated.—of the murther of the
late lord there is no doubt, the criminal hath
confeſſed it, and the circumſtances confirm it.
—the proofs of his crime are ſo connected with
thoſe of the young man's birth, that one cannot be publick without the other.—we are
deſirous to do juſtice, and yet are unwilling,
for the lord Fitz-Owen's ſake, to bring the
criminal to publick ſhame and puniſhment.—
we wiſh to find out a medium, we therefore
deſire ſir Philip to make propoſals for his ward,
and let lord Fitz-Owen anſwer for himſelf and
his brother, and we will be moderators between
them.—here every one expreſſed approbation,
and called upon ſir Philip to make his demands.

If, ſaid he, I were to demand ſtrict juſtice,
I ſhould not be ſatisfied with any thing leſs
than the life of the criminal, but I am a chriſtian ſoldier, the diſciple of him who came into
the world to ſave ſinners; for his ſake, ſaid
he, (croſſing himſelf) I forego my revenge, I
ſpare the guilty; if heaven gives him time for
repentance, man ſhould not deny it; it is my
ward's particular requeſt. that I will not bring
ſhame upon the houſe of his benefactor, the
lord Fitz-Owen, for whom he hath a filial affection and profound veneration.—my propoſals

O 3   are

are thefe ; firft, that the criminal make reftitution of the title and eftate obtained with fo
much injuftice and cruelty to the lawful heir,
whom he fhall acknowledge fuch before proper witnefles.—fecondly, that he fhall furrender his own lawful inheritance and perfonal
eftate into the hands of the lord Fitz-Owen,
in truft for his fons, who are his heirs of blood.
Thirdly, that he fhall retire into a religious
houfe, or elfe quit the kingdom in three months
time, and in either cafe, thofe who enjoy his
fortune fhall allow him a decent annuity, that
he may not want the comforts of life.—by the
laft 1 difable him from the means of doing further mifchief, and enable him to devote the
remainder of his days to penitence.—thefe are
my propofals, and I give him four and twenty
hours to confider of them: if he refufes to
comply with them, I fhall be obliged to proceed to feverer meafures, and to a publick
profecution ; but the goodnefs of the lord
Fitz-Owen, bid me expect from his influence
with his brother, a compliance with propofals,
made out of refpect to his honourable character.

Lord Graham applauded the humanity, prudence and piety of fir Philip's propofals.—he
enforced them with all his influence and eloquence.—lord Clifford feconded him, and the
reft gave tokens of approbation.—fir Robert
Fitz-Owen then rofe up.—I beg leave to obferve to the company, who are going to difpofe fo generoufly of another man's property,
that my father purchafed the caftle and eftate
of the houfe of Lovel; who is to repay him
the money for it?

Sir

Sir Philip then said, I have also a question to ask.—who is to pay the arrears of my ward's estate, which he has unjustly been kept out of these one and twenty years?—let lord Clifford answer to both points, for he is not interested in either?—lord Clifford smiled.—I think the first question is answered by the second, and that the parties concerned should set one against the other, especially as lord Fitz-Owen's children will inherit the fortune, which includes the purchase money.—lord Graham said this determination is both equitable and generous, and I hope will answer the expectations on all sides.— sir Philip said, I have another proposal to make to my lord Fitz-Owen, but I first wait for the acceptance of those already made.—lord Fitz-Owen said, I shall report them to my brother, and acquaint the company with his resolution to-morrow.

They then separated, and the baron with his sons returned to the sick man's chamber, there he exhorted his brother, with the piety of a confessor, to repent of his sins and make atonement for them.—he made known sir Philip's proposals, and observed on the wonderful discovery of his crime, and the punishment that followed it; your repentance may be accepted, and your crime may yet be pardoned; if you continue refractory and refuse to make atonement, you will draw down upon you a severer punishment.—the criminal would not confess, and yet could not deny the truth and justice of his observations.—he spent several hours in his brother's chamber, he sent for the priest who took his confession, and they both sat up in the chamber all night, advising, persuading, and

exhorting

exhorting him to do juſtice, and to comply with the propoſals.—he was unwilling to give up the world, and yet more ſo to become the object of publick ſhame, diſgrace and puniſhment.

The next day lord Fitz-Owen ſummoned the company into his brother's chamber, and there declared in his name, that he accepted ſir Philip Harclay's propoſals, that if the young man could, as he promiſed, direct them to the places were his parents were buried, and if his birth ſhould be authenticated by his foſter parents, he ſhould be acknowledged the heir of the houſe of Lovel.—that to be certified of theſe things, they muſt commiſſion proper perſons to go with him for this purpoſe; and in caſe the truth ſhould be made plain, they ſhould immediately put him in poſſeſſion of the caſtle and eſtate, in the ſtate it was.—he deſired lord Graham and lord Clifford to chooſe the commiſſioners, and gave ſir Philip and Edmund a right to add to them each another perſon.

Lord Graham named the eldeſt ſon of lord Clifford, and the other in return named his nephew; they alſo chooſe the prieſt, lord Graham's confeſſor, and the eldeſt ſon of baron Fitz-Owen, to his great mortification.——ſir Philip appointed mr. William Fitz-Owen, and Edmund choſe father Oſwald—they choſe out the ſervants to attend them, who were alſo to be witneſſes of all that ſhould paſs.—lord Clifford propoſed to baron Fitz-Owen, that as ſoon as the commiſſioners were ſet out, the remainder of the company ſhould adjourn to his ſeat in Cumberland, whither lord Graham ſhould be invited to accompany them, and to ſtay

till

till this affair was decided,—after some debate this was agreed to, and at the same time, that the criminal should be kept with them till every thing was properly settled.

Lord Fitz-Owen gave his son William the charge to receive and entertain the commissioners at the castle; but before they set out sir Philip had a conference with lord Fitz-Owen concerning the surrender of the castle, sir Philip insisted on the furniture and stock of the farm in consideration of the arrears.—lord Fitz-Owen slightly mentioned the young man's education and expences.—sir Philip answered, you are right my lord, I had not thought of this point; we owe you in this respect more than we can ever repay, but you know not half the respect and affection Edmund bears for you, when restitution of his title and fortune are fully made, his happiness will still depend on you.—how on me, said the baron.—why he will not be happy unless you honour him with your notice and esteem; but this is not all, I must hope that you will do still more for him.—indeed! said the baron, he has put my regard for him to a severe proof, what further can he expect from me?—my dear lord be not offended, I have only one more proposal to make to you, if you refuse it, I can allow for you, and I confess it requires greatness of mind, but not more than you possess to grant it.—well sir, speak your demand?—say rather my request.—it is this.—cease to look upon Edmund as the enemy of your house, look upon him as a son, and make him so indeed! how say you sir Philip? my son!—yes my lord, give him your daughter, he is already

your

your fon in filial affection ; your fon William
and he are fworn brothers, what remains but
to make him yours, he deferves fuch a parent,
you fuch a fon, and you will ingraft into your
family, the name, title and eftate of Lovel,
which will be entailed on your pofterity for
ever.—this offer requires much confideration,
faid the baron.—fuffer me to fuggeft fome to
you, faid fir Philip; this match is, I think
verily, pointed out by providence, which hath
conducted the dear boy through fo many dan-
gers, and brought him within view of his happi-
piness ; look on him as the precious relick of
a noble houfe, the fon of my deareft friend! or
look on him as my fon and heir, and let me as
his father, implore you to confent to his marriage with your daughter ?—the baron's heart
was touched, he turned away his face.——oh
fir Philip Harclay, what a friend are you!—
why fhould fuch a man be our enemy?——
my lord, faid fir Philip, we are not, cannot be
enemies, our hearts are already allied, and I
am certain we fhall one day be dear friends.
the baron fuppreffed his emotions, but fir
Philip faw into his heart.—I muft confult my
eldeft fon, faid he.—then faid he, I forefee
much difficulty, he is prejudiced againft Edmund, and thinks the reftitution of his inheritance an injury to your family, hereafter he
will fee this alliance in a different light, and
will rejoice that fuch a brother is added to the
family, but at prefent he will fet his face a-
gainft it ; however we will not defpair, virtue
and refolution will furmount all obftacles, let
me call in young Lovel.

He

He brought Edmund to the baron, and acquainted him with the propofal he had been making in his name, my lord's anfwers and the objections he feared on the part of fir Robert.—Edmund kneeled to the baron, he took his hand and preffed it to his lips.—beft of men! of parents! of patrons! faid he, I will ever be your fon in filial affection, whether I have the honour to be legally fo or not; not one of your own children can feel a ftronger fenfe of love and duty.—tell me, faid the baron, do you love my daughter?—I do my lord, with the moft ardent affection, I never loved any woman but her, and if I am fo unfortunate as to be refufed her, I will not marry at all.—oh my lord, reject not my honeft fuit! your alliance will give me confequence with myfelf, it will excite me to act worthy of the ftation to which I am exalted; if you refufe me, I fhall feem an abject wretch, difdained by thofe whom my heart claims relation to, your family are the whole world to me.—give me your lovely daughter! give me alfo your fon, my beloved William! and let me fhare with them the fortune providence beftows upon me, but what is title or fortune, if I am deprived of the fociety of thofe I love?

Edmund, faid the baron, you have a noble friend, but you have a ftronger in my heart, which I think was implanted there by heaven to aid its own purpofes; I feel a variety of emotions of different kinds, and am afraid to truft my own heart with you; but anfwer me a queftion? are you affured of my daughter's confent? have you folicited her favour? have you gained her affections?—never my lord! I

am

am incapable of so base an action; I have loved her at an humble distance, but in my situation I should have thought it a violation of all the laws of gratitude and hospitality, to have presumed to speak the sentiments of my heart.—then you have acted with unquestionable honour on this, and I must say on all other occasions.—your approbation my lord is the first wish of my life, it is the seal of my honour and happiness.

Sir Philip smiled.—my lord Fitz-Owen, I am jealous of Edmund's preferable regard for you, it is just the same now as formerly.——Edmund came to sir Philip, he threw himself into his arms, he wept, he was overpowered with the feelings of his heart, he prayed to heaven to strengthen his mind to support bis inexpressible sensations!——I am overwhelmed with obligations, said he, oh best of friends, teach me like you, to make my actions speak for me!—enough Edmund, I know your heart, and that is my security.—my lord speak to him, and bring him to himself by behaving coldly to him if you can.—the baron said, I must not trust myself with you, you make a child of me! I will only add, gain my son Robert's favour, and be assured of mine; I owe some respect to the heir of my family, he is brave, honest and sincere; your enemies are separated from him, you have William's influence in your behalf, make one effort and let me know the result.—Edmund kissed his hand in transports of joy and gratitude —I will not lose a moment, said he, I fly to obey your commands.

Edmund went immediately to his friend William and related all that had passed between
the

the baron, fir Philip and himfelf.—William
promifed him his intereft in the warmed manner, he recapitulated all that had paffed in the
caftle fince his departure, but he guarded his
fifter's delicacy, till it fhould be refolved to
give way to his addrefs.—they both confulted
young Clifford, who had conceived an affection
to Edmund for his amiable qualities, and to
William for his generous friendfhip for him.—
he promifed them his affiftance, as fir Robert
feemed defirous to cultivate his friendfhip.—
accordingly they both attacked him with the
whole artillery of friendfhip and perfuafion.—
Clifford urged the merits of Edmund, and the
advantages of his alliance.—William enforced
his arguments by a retrofpect of Edmund's paft
life, and obferved that every obftacle thrown
in his way, had brought his enemies to fhame,
and increafe of honour to himfelf.—I fay nothing of his noble qualities and affectionate
heart, thofe who have been fo many years
his companions, can want no proofs of it.—we
know your attachment to him fir, faid fir Robert, and in confequence your partiality.—nay,
faid William, you are fenfible of the truth of
my affertions, and I am confident would have
loved him yourfelf, but for the infinuations of
his enemies; but if he fhould make good his affertions, even you muft be convinced of his veracity.—and you would have my father give
him your fifter upon this uncertainty?—no fir,
but upon thefe conditions.—but fuppofe he does
not make them good?—then I will be of your
party, and give up his intereft.—very well fir,
my father may do as he pleafes, but I cannot
agree to give my fifter to one who has always

P   ftood

ftood in the way of our family, and now turns us out of our own houfe.

I am forry brother, you fee his pretenfions in fo wrong a light, but if you think there is any impofture in the cafe, go with us and be a witnefs of all that paffes ?—no, not I !—if Edmund is to be mafter of the caftle, I will never more fet my foot in it.—this matter, faid mr. Clifford, muft be left to time, which has brought ftranger things to pafs.—fir Robert's honour and good fenfe will enable him to fubdue his prejudices, and to judge impartially.—they took leave, and went to make preparations for their journey.

Edmund made his report of fir Robert's inflexibility to his father, in prefence of fir Philip, who again ventured to urge the baron on his favourite fubject.—it becomes me to wait for the further proofs, faid he, but if they are as clear as I expect, I will not be inexorable to your wifhes; fay nothing more on this fubject till the return of the commiffioners.——they were profufe in their acknowldgements of his goodnefs.

Edmund took a tender leave of his two paternal friends; when, faid he, I take poffeffion of my inheritance, I muft hope for the company of you both to compleat my happinefs.—of me, faid fir Philip, you may be certain, and as far as my influence reaches, of the baron.—he was filent.—Edmund affured them of his conftant prayers for their happinefs.

Soon after the commiffioners, with Edmund, fet out for Lovel caftle, and the following day the lord Clifford fet out for his own houfe, with baron Fitz-Owen and his fon.—the nominal

baron

baron was carried with them, very much
againſt his will.—ſir Philip Harclay was invited
to go with them by lord Clifford, who declared
his preſence neceſſary to bring things to a
concluſion; they all joined in acknowledging
their obligations to lord Graham's generous
hoſpitality, they beſought him to accompany
them, and at length he conſented, on condition they would allow him to go to and fro,
as his duty ſhould call him.

Lord Clifford received them with the greateſt
hoſpitality, and preſented them to his lady and
three daughters, who were in the bloom of
youth and beauty; they ſpent their time very
pleaſantly, excepting the criminal, who continued gloomy and reſerved, and declined
company.

In the mean time the commiſſioners proceeded on their journey; when they were within a day's diſtance from the caſtle, mr. William
and his ſervant put forward, and arrived ſeveral
hours before the reſt, to make preparations for
their reception.—his ſiſter and brother received
them with open arms, and enquired eagerly
after the event of the journey to the north.—
he gave them a brief account of every thing
that had happened to their uncle; adding, but
this is not all.— ſir Philip Harclay has brought
a young man, whom he pretends is the ſon of
the late lord Lovel, and claims his eſtate and
title.—this perſon is on his journey hither,
with ſeveral others who are commiſſioned to
enquire into certain particulars, to confirm his
pretenſions; if he makes good his claim, my
father will ſurrender the caſtle and eſtate into
his hands, ſir Philip and my lord have many

points

points to settle, and he has proposed a compromise that you, my sister, ought to know, because it nearly concerns you.—me brother William, pray explain yourself?—why, he proposes that in lieu of arrears and other expectations, my father shall give his dear Emma to the heir of Lovel, in full of all demands.—she changed colour.—holy Mary! said she.—does my father agree to this proposal?—he is not very averse to it, but sir Robert refuses his consent; but I have given him my interest with you.—have you indeed?——what a stranger, perhaps an impostor, who comes to turn us out of our dwelling?—have patience my Emma! see this young man without prejudice, and perhaps you will like him as well as I do.—I am surprized at you William!—dear Emma I cannot bear to see you uneasy; think of the man who of all others you would wish to see in a situation to ask you of your father, and expect to see your wishes reallized.—impossible, said she!—nothing is impossible. my dear; let us be prudent, and all will end happily; you must help me to receive and entertain these commissioners.—I expect a very solemn scene, but when that is once got over, happier hours than the past will succeed; we shall first visit the haunted apartment, you my sister will keep in your own till I shall send for you.—I go now to give orders to the servants.—he went and ordered them to be in waiting, and himself and his youngest brother stood in readiness to receive them.

The sound of the horn announced the arrival of the commissioners, at the same instant a sudden gust of wind arose, and the outward gates flew open,—they entered the court-yard,

and

ard the great folding doors into the hall were opened without any affiftance.—the moment Edmund entered the hall, every door in the houfe flew open, the fervants all rufhed into the hall, and fear was written on their countenances; Jofeph only was undaunted.—thefe doors, faid he, open of their own aecord to receive their mafter!—this is he indeed!—Edmund was foon apprized of what had happened. —I accept the omen, faid he.—gentlemen let us go forward to the apartment!—let us finifh the work of fate!—I will lead the way; he went on to the apartment, followed by all prefent.—open the fhutters, faid he, the day-light fhall no longer be excluded here; the deeds of darknefs fhall now be brought to light.

They defcended the ftaircafe, every door was open, till they came to the fatal clofet.— Edmund called to mr. William.—approach my friend, and behold the door your family overlooked!—they came forward, he drew the key out of his bofom and unlocked the door, he made them obferve that the boards were all loofe; he then called to the fervants, and bid them remove every thing out of the clofet.— while they were doing this, Edmund fhewed them the breaft plate all ftained with blood.— he then called to Jofeph.—do you know whofe was this fuit of armour?—it was my lord's, faid Jofeph, the late lord Lovel, I have feen him wear it.

Edmund bad them bring fhovels and remove the earth.—while they were gone he defired Ofwald to repeat all that paffed the night they fat up together in that apartment, which he did, till the fervants returned.—they threw out the earth while the by-standers in solemn silence waited the event.—after some time and labour they struck against something.—they proceeded till they discovered a large trunk, which with some difficulty they drew out.—it had been corded round, but the cords were rotted to dust.—they opened it and found a skeleton which appeared to have been tied neck and heels together, and forced into the trunk. —behold, said Edmund, the bones of him to whom I owe my birth!—the priest from lord Graham's advanced.—this is undoubtedly the body of the lord Lovel, I heard his kinsman confess the manner in which he was interred. —let this awful spectacle be a lesson to all present! that though wickedness may triumph for a season, a day of retribution will come.—Oswald exclaimed, behold the day of retribution! of triumph to the innocent, of shame and confusion to the wicked:

The young gentlemen declared that Edmund had made good his assertions, what then said they, remains?—I propose, said lord Graham's priest, that an account be written of this discovery, and signed by all the witnesses present, that an attested copy be left in the hands of this gentleman, and the original be sent to the barons and sir Philip Harclay, to convince them of the truth of it.

Mr. Clifford then desired Edmund to proceed in his own way.—the first thing I propose to do is, to have a coffin made for these honoured remains, I trust to find the bones of my other parent, and to inter them altogether in consecrated ground.—unfortunate pair! you shall at last rest together! your son shall pay the last du‑

ties to your aſhes!—he ſtopped to ſhed tears,
and none preſent but paid this tribute to their
misfortunes.—Edmund recovered his voice and
proceeded.—my next requeſt is, that father
Oſwald and this reverend father, with whoever
elſe the gentlemen ſhall appoint, will ſend for
Andrew and Margery Twyford, and examine
them concerning the circumſtances of my birth,
and the death and burial of my unfortunate mother.—it ſhall be done, ſaid mr. William, but
firſt let me intreat you to come with me and
take ſome refreſhment after your journey, for
you muſt be fatigued; after dinner we will
proceed in the enquiry.

They all followed him into the great hall,
where they were entertained with great hoſpitality, and mr. William did the honours in
his father's name.—Edmund's heart was deeply
affected, and the ſolemnity of his deportment
bore witneſs to his ſincerity, but it was a manly
ſorrow, that did not make him neglect his duty
to his friends or himſelf.—he enquired after the
health of the lady Emma.—ſhe is well, ſaid
William, and as much your friend as ever.—
Edmund bowed in ſilence.

After dinner the commiſſioners ſent for Andrew and his wife; they examined them ſeparately, and found their accounts agreed together, and were in ſubſtance the ſame as Oſwald
and Edmund had before related, ſeparately
alſo.—the commiſſioners obſerved, that there
could be no colluſion between them, and that
the proofs were indiſputable.—they kept the
foſter parents all night, and the next day Andrew
directed them to the place where the lady Lovel
was buried, between two trees which he had
marked

marked for a memorial.—they collected the bones and carried them to the castle, where Edmund caused a stately coffin to be made for the remains of the unfortunate pair.—the two priests obtained leave to look in the coffin buried in the church, and found nothing but stones and earth in it.—the commissioners then declared they were fully satisfied of the reallity of Edmund's pretensions.

The two priests were employed in drawing up a circumstantial account of these discoveries, in order to make their report to the barons at their return.—in the mean time mr. William took an opportunity to introduce Edmund to his sister.—my Emma, said he, the heir of Lovel is desirous to pay his respects to you.— they were both in apparent confusion, but Edmund's wore off, and Emma's increased. I have been long desirous, said he, to pay my respects to the lady whom I most honour, but unavoidable duties have detained me, when these are fully paid, it is my wish to devote the remainder of my life to lady Emma!—are you then the heir of Lovel?—I am madam, and am also the man in whose behalf I once presumed to speak.—'tis very strange indeed!—it is so madam to myself, but time that reconciles us to all things, will, I hope, render this change in my situation familiar to you.—William said, you are both well acquainted with the wishes of my heart, but my advice is, that you do not encourage a farther intimacy till my lord's determination be fully known.—you may dispose of me as you please, said Edmund, but I cannot help declaring my wishes, yet I will submit to my lord's sentence, though he should doom me to despair.   From.

From this period, the young pair behaved with folenm reſpeſt to each other, but with apparent reſerve.—the young lady ſometimes appeared in company, but oftener choſe to be in her own apartment, where ſhe began to believe and hope for the completion ot her wiſhes.—the uncertainty of the baron's determination, threw an air ot anxiety over Edmund's face.—his friend William, by the moſt tender care and attentions, ſtrove to diſpel his fears, and encourage his hopes, but he waited with impatience for the return of the commiſſioners, and the deciſion of his fate.

While theſe things paſſed at the caſtle of Lovel, the nominal baron recovered his health and ſtrength at the houſe of lord Clifford.—in the ſame proportion he grew more and more ſhy and reſerved, avoided the company ot his brother and nephew, and was frequently ſhut up with his twoſervants.—ſir Robert Fitz-Owen made ſeveral attempts to gain his confidence, but in vain ; he was equally ſhy to him as the reſt. —M. Zadiſky obſerved his motions with the penetration for which his countrymen have been diſtinguiſhed in all ages.—he communicated his ſuſpicions to ſir Philip and the barons, giving it as his opinion that the criminal was meditating an eſcape.—they aſked what he thought was to be done ?—Zadiſky offered to watch him in turn with another perſon, and to lye in wait for him.—he alſo propoſed that horſes ſhould be kept in readineſs, and men to mount them, without knowledge of the ſervice they were to be employed in.—the barons agreed to leave the whole management of this affair to Zadiſky.—he took his meaſures ſo well,

well, that he intercepted the three fugitives in
the fields adjoining to the houfe, and brought
all three back priioners.—they confined them
feparately, while the lords and gentlemen confulted how to difpofe of them.

Sir Philip applied to lord Fitz-Owen, he begged leave to be filent.—I have nothing, faid
he, to offer in favour of this bad man, and I
cannot propofe harfher meafures with fo near
a relation.—Zadifky then begged to be heard.
—you can have no longer any reliance upon
the word of a man who has forfeited all pretenfions to honour and fincerity; I have long
wifhed to revifit once more my native country,
and to enquire after fome very dear friends I
left there; I will undertake to convey this man
to a very diftant part of the world, where it
will be out of his power to do further mifchief,
and free his relations from an ungrateful
charge, unlefs you fhould rather choofe to bring
him to punifhment here.—lord Clifford approved of the propofal, lord Fitz-Owen remained filent, but fhowed no marks of difapprobation.

Sir Philip objected to parting with his friend,
but Zadifky affured him he had particular reafons for returning to the holy land, of which
he fhould be judge hereafter.—fir Philip defired
the lord Fitz-Owen to give him his company
to the criminal's apartment, faying, we will
have one more converfation with him, and that
fhall decide his fate.—they found him filent
and fullen, and he refufed to anfwer their queftions.—fir Philp then befpoke him.—after the
proofs you have given of your fallehood and
infincerity, we can no longer have any reliance
upon you, nor faith in your fulfilling the conditions

ditions of our agreement; I will therefore once more make you a proposal that shall still leave you indebted to our clemency; you shall banish yourself from England for ever, and go in pilgrimage to the holy land, with such companions as we shall appoint.—or secondly, you shall enter directly into a monastry, and there be shut up for life.—or thirdly, if you refuse both these offers, I will go directly to court, thrown myself at the feet of my sovereign, relate the whole story of your wicked life and actions, and demand vengeance on your head.—the king is too good and pious to let such villany go unpunished; he will bring you to public shame and punishment; and be you assured if I begin this prosecution, I will pursue it to the utmost.—I appeal to your worthy brother for the justice of my proceeding.—I reason no more with you, I only declare my resolution.—I wait your answer one hour, and the next I put in execution whatever you shall oblige me to determine.—so saying they retired, and left him to reflect and to resolve.—at the expiration of the hour they sent Zadisky to receive his answer.—he insinuated to him the generosity and charity of sir Philip and the lords, and the certainty of their resolutions, and begged him to take care what answer he returned, for that his fate depended on it.—he kept silent several minutes, resentment and despair were painted on his visage.—at length he spoke.

Tell my proud enemies that I prefer banishment to death, infamy, or a life of solitude.—you have chosen well, said Zadisky, to a wise man all countries are alike, it shall be my care to make mine agreeable to you.—are

you

you then the perfon chofen for my companion?—I am fir, and you may judge by that circumftance, that thofe whom you call your enemies, are not fo in effect.—farewel fir, I go to prepare for our departure.

Zaditky went and made his report, and then fet immediately about his preparations.——he chofe two active young men for his attendants, and gave them directions to keep a ftrict eye upon their charge, for that they fhould be accountable if he fhould efcape them.

In the mean time the baron Fitz-Owen had feveral conferences with his brother, he endeavoured to make him fenfible of his crimes, and of the juftice and clemency of his conqueror, but he was moody and referved to him as to the reft.—fir Philip Harclay obliged him to furrender his worldly eftates into the hands of lord Fitz-Owen.—a writing was drawn up for that purpofe, and executed in the prefence of them all.—lord Fitz-Owen engaged to allow him an annual fum, and to advance money for the expences of his voyage.—he fpoke to him in the moft affectionate manner, but he refufed his embrace.—you will have nothing to regret, faid he, haughtily, for the gain is yours.-fir Philip conjured Zaditky to return to him again.—he anfwered, I will either return, or give fuch reafons for my ftay, as you fhall approve.—I will fend a meffenger to acquaint you with my arrival in Syria, and with fuch other particulars as I fhall judge interefting to you and yours.— in the mean time remember me in your prayers, and preferve for me thofe fentiments of friendfhip and efteem, that I have always deemed one of the chief honours and bleffings of my life.—

life.—commend my love and duty to your adopted son, he will more than supply my absence, and be the comfort of your old age.—adieu, best and noblest of friends!—they took a tender leave of each other, not without tears on both sides.

. The travellers set out directly for a distant sea port, where they heard of a ship bound for. the Levant, in which they embarked and proceeded on their voyage.

. The commissioners arrived at lord Clifford's a few days after the departure of the adventurers; they gave a minute account of their commission, and expressed themselves entirely satisfied of the justice of Edmund's pretensions; they gave an account in writing of all that they had been eye witness to, and ventured to. urge the baron Fitz-Owen on the subject of Edmund's wishes.—the baron was already disposed in his favour, his mind was employed in. the future establishment of his family.—during their residence at lord Clifford's, his eldest son sir Robert had cast his eye upon the eldest daughter of that nobleman, and he besought his father to ask her in marriage for him.—— the baron was pleased with the alliance, and took the first opportunity to mention it to lord Clifford; who answered him pleasantly.——I will give my daughter to your son, upon condition that you will give yours to the heir of Lovel.—the baron looked serious.—lord Clifford went on.—I like that young man so well, that I would accept him for a son-in-law, if he asked me for my daughter, and if I have any influence with you I will use it in his behalf.—a powerful solicitor indeed! said the

Q   baron.

baron.—but you know my eldeſt ſon's relucﬁ
tance to it; if he conſents, ſo will I.—he ſhall
conſent, ſaid lord Clifford, or he ſhall have
no daughter of mine.—let him ſubdue his prejudices, and then I will lay aſide my ſcruples.
—but my lord, if I can obtain his free conſent,
it will be beſt for all.—I will try once more,
if he will not, I will leave it wholly to your
management.

When the noble company were all aſſembled,
ſir Philip Harclay revived the ſubject, and beſought the lord Fitz-Owen to put an end to the
work he had begun, by confirming Edmund's
happineſs——the baron roſe up and thus ſpoke.
—the proofs of Edmund's noble birth, the ſtill
ſtronger ones of his excellent endowments and
qualities; the ſolicitations of ſo many noble
friends in his behalf, have altogether determined me in his favour, and I hope to do juſtice to his merit, without detriment to my
other children; I am reſolved to make them
all as happy as my power will allow me to do;
lord Clifford has been ſo gracious to promiſe
his fair daughter to my ſon Robert, upon certain conditions, that I will take upon me to
ratify, and which will render my ſon worthy
of the happineſs that awaits him; my children
are the undoubted heirs of my unhappy brother
Lovel, you my ſon ſhall immediately take
poſſeſſion of your uncle's houſe and eſtate, only
obliging you to pay to each of your younger
brothers, the ſum of one thouſand pounds;
on this condition I will ſecure that eſtate to you
and your heirs for ever! I will by my own act
and deed, ſurrender the caſtle and eſtate of
Lovel to the right owner, and at the ſame time
marry

marry him to my daughter: I will settle a proper allowance upon my two younger sons, and dispose of what remains by a will and testament, and then I shall have done all my business in this world, and shall have nothing to do but prepare for the next.

Oh my father! said sir Robert, I cannot bear your generosity! you would give away all to others, and reserve nothing for yourself.—not so my son, said the baron.—I will repair my old castle in Wales, and reside there.—I will visit my children, and be visited by them; I will enjoy their happiness, and by that means increase my own; whether I look backwards or forwards I shall have nothing to do but rejoice, and be thankful to heaven that has given me so many blessings; I shall have the comfortable reflections of having discharged my duties as a citizen, a husband, a father, a friend, and whenever I am summoned away from this world, I shall die content.

Sir Robert came forward with tears on his cheeks, he kneeled to his father.—best of parents, and of men! said he, you have subdued a heart that has been too refractory to your will; you have this day made me sensible how much I owe to your goodness and forbearance with me; forgive me all that is past, and from henceforward dispose of me, I will have no will but yours, no ambition but to be worthy of the name of your son.—and this day, said the baron, do I enjoy the true happiness of a father! rise my son, and take possession of the first place in my affection without reserve.—they embraced with tears on both sides.—the company rose and congratulated both father

and

and son.—the baron presented his son to lord
Clifford, who embraced him, and said, you
shall have my daughter, for I see that you deserve her.

Sir Philip Harclay approached.—the baron
gave his son's hand to the knight.—love and
respect that good man, said he, deserve his
friendship, and you will obtain it.—nothing but
congratulations were heard on all sides.

When their joy was in some degree, reduced
to composure, sir Philip proposed that they
should begin to execute the schemes of happiness they had planned.—he proposed that my
lord Fitz-Owen should go with him to the castle
of Lovel and settle the family there.—the baron
consented, and both together invited such of
the company as liked it, to accompany them
thither.—a nephew of lord Graham's, another
of lord Clifford's, two gentlemen, friends of
sir Philip Harclay, several of his dependants
and domesticks; father Oswald and the attendants on the rest.—lord Fitz-Owen gave orders
for their speedy departure.—lord Graham and
his friends took leave of them in order to return to his own home; but before he went,
he engaged his eldest nephew and heir to the second daughter of the lord Clifford.—sir Robert
offered himself to the eldest, who modestly received his address, and made no objection to
his proposal.—the fathers confirmed their engagement.

Lord Fitz-Owen promised to return to the
celebration of the marriage, in the mean time
he ordered his son to go and take possession of
his uncle's house, and to settle his household;
he invited young Clifford and some other gentlemen

tlemen to go with him.—the company separated with regret, and with many promises of friendship on all sides, and the gentlemen of the north were to cultivate the good neighbourhood on both sides of the borders.

Sir Philip Harclay and the baron Fitz-Owen, with their friends and attendants set forwards for the castle of Lovel; a servant went before at full speed to acquaint the family of their approach.—Edmund was in great anxiety of mind, now the crisis of his fate was near at hand.—he enquired of the messenger who were of the party, and finding that sir Philip Harclay was there, and that sir Robert Fitz-Owen staid in the north, his hopes rose above his fears.—mr. William, attended by a servant, rode forward to meet them; he desired Edmund to stay and receive them.—he was under some difficulty with regard to his behaviour to the lovely Emma ; a thousand times his heart rose to his lips, as often he suppressed his emotions. —they both sighed frequently, said little, thought much, and wished for the event.—— master Walter was too young to partake of their anxieties, but he wished for the arrival of his father to end them.

Mr. William's impatience spurred him on to meet his father.—as soon as he saw him, he rode up directly to him.—my dear father, you are welcome home ! said he.—I think not sir, said the baron, and looked serious.—why so my lord? said William.—because it is no longer mine, but another man's home, answered he, and I must receive my welcome from him. —meaning Edmund?— said William, whom else can it be?—ah my lord ! he is your creature,

ture, your fervant, he puts his fate into your
hands, and will fubmit to your pleafure in all
things!—why comes he not to meet us? faid
the baron.—his fears prevent him, faid William, but fpeak the word and I will fetch him ?
—no, faid the baron, we will wait on him.—
William looked confufed.—is Edmund fo unfortunate, faid he, as to have incurred your
difpleafure?—fir Philip Harclay advanced, and
laid his hand on William's faddle.—generous
impatience! noble youth! faid he, look round
you, and fee if you can difcover in this company one enemy of your friend? leave to your
excellent father the time and manner of explaining himfelf, he only can do juftice to his
own fentiments.—the baron fmiled on fir Philip.—William's countenance cleared up, they
went forward and foon arrived at the caftle of
Lovel.

Edmund was walking to and fro in the hall,
when he heard the horn that announced their
arrival, his emotions were fo great that he
could hardly fupport them.—the baron and fir
Philip entered the hall hand in hand; Edmund
threw himfelf at their feet and embraced their
knees, but could not utter a word.—they raifed
him between them, and ftrove to encourage
him, but he threw himfelf into the arms of fir
Philip Harclay, deprived of ftrength, and almoft of life.—they fupported him to a feat,
where he recovered by degrees, but had no
power to fpeak his feelings.—he looked up to
his benefactors in the moft affecting manner,
he laid his hand upon his bofom, but was ftill
filent.—compofe yourfelf my dear fon, faid fir
Philip, you are in the arms of your beft friends,

look

look up to the happiness that awaits you, enjoy the blessings that heaven sends you, lift up your heart in gratitude to the Creator, and think less of what you owe to the creature! you will have time enough to pay us your acknowledgements hereafter.

The company came round them, the servants flocked into the hall, shouts of joy were heard on all sides, the baron came and took Edmund's hand.—rise sir, said he, and do the honours of your house! it is yours from this day, we are your guests, and expect from you our welcome!—Edmund kneeled to the baron, he spoke with a faltering voice.—my lord I am yours! all that I have is at your devotion!—dispose of me as it pleases you best.—the baron embraced him with the greatest affection, look round you, said he, and salute yo friends, these gentlemen came hither to do ou honour.—Edmund revived, he embraced and welcomed the gentlemen.—father Oswald received his embrace with peculiar affection, and gave him his benediction in a most affecting manner.—Edmund exclaimed, pray for me father! that I may bear all these blessings with gratitude and moderation!—he then saluted and shook hand with all the servants, not omitting the meanest.—he distinguished Joseph by a cordial embrace, he called him his dear friend.—now, said he, I can return your friendship, and I am proud to acknowledge it!—the old man with a faltering voice cried out.—now I have lived long enough! I have seen my master's son acknowledged for the heir of Lovel! the hall ecchoed with his words.—long live the heir of Lovel!

The

The baron took Edmund's hands in his own.
—let us retire from this croud, said he, we
have bufinefs of a more private nature to tranf-
act.—he led to the parlour, followed by fir
Philip and the other gentlemen.—where are
my other children, faid he ?—William retired
and prefently returned with his brother and
fifter.—they kneeled to their father, who
raifed and embraced them.—he then called
out, William!—Edmund!—come and receive
my blefling alfo.—they approached hand in
hand, they kneeled, and he gave them a folemn benediction.—your friendfhip deferves
our praife, my children! love each other always! and may heaven pour down its choiceft
bleflings upon your heads!—they rofe and embraced in filent raptures of joy.—Edmund prefented his friend to fir Philip.—I underftand
you, faid he, this gentleman was my firft ac-
quaintance of this family, he has a title to
the fecond place in my heart, I fhall tell him
at more leifure how much I love and honour
him for his own fake as well as yours.——he
embraced the youth, and defired his friendfhip.

Come hither my Emma! faid the baron.—
fhe approached with tears on her cheek,
fweetly blufhing, like the damafk rofe, wet
with the dew of the morning.—I muft afk you
a ferious queftion my child, anfwer me with
the fame fincerity you would to heaven ?—you
fee this young man, the heir of Lovel! you
have known him long, confult your own heart,
and tell me whether you have any objection
to receive him for your hufband ?—I have promifed to all this company to give you to him,
but upon condition that you approve him; I
think

think him worthy of you, and whether you accept him or not, he ſhall ever be to me a ſon, but heaven forbid that I ſhould compel my child to give her hand where ſhe cannot beſtow her heart; ſpeak freely, and decide this point for me and for yourſelf?—the fair Emma bluſhed and was under ſome confuſion. —her virgin modeſty prevented her ſpeaking for ſome moments.—Edmund trembled, he leaned upon William's ſhoulder to ſupport himſelf.—the fair Emma caſt her eye upon him, ſhe ſaw his emotion and haſtened to relieve him.—ſhe ſpoke in a ſoft voice which gathered ſtrength as ſhe proceeded.—my lord and father's goodneſs has always prevented my wiſhes; I am the happieſt of all children, in being able to obey his commands, without offering violence to my own inclinations; as I am called upon in this publick manner, it is but juſtice to this gentleman's merit to declare, that were I at liberty to chooſe a huſband from all the world, he only ſhould be my choice, who I can ſay with joy is my father's alſo.— Edmund bowed low, he advanced towards her.—the baron took his daughter's hand, and preſented it to him.—he kneeled upon one kneé, he took her hand, kiſſed it, and preſſed it to his boſom.—the baron embraced and bleſſed them.—he preſented them to ſir Philip Harclay.——receive and acknowledge your children, ſaid he!—I do receive them as the gift of heaven! ſaid the noble knight, they are as much mine as if I had begotten them; all that I have is theirs, and ſhall deſcend to their children for ever.—a freſh ſcene of congratulation enſued, and the hearts of all the

auditors

auditors were too much engaged, to be able foon to return to the eafe and tranquility of common life,

After they had refrefhed themfelves, and recovered from the emotions they had fuftained on this interefting occafion.—Edmund thus addreffed the baron.—on the brink of happi- nefs I muft claim your attention to a melan- choly fubject; the bones of both my parents lie unburied in this houfe, permit me, my hon- oured lord, to perform my laft duties to them, and the remainder of my life fhall be devoted to you and yours.—certainly, faid the baron, why have you not interred them?—my lord I waited for your arrival, that you might be cer- tified of the reallity, and that no doubts might remain.—I have no doubts, faid the baron.— alas, both the crime and punifhment of the offender leave no room for them!—he fighed. —let us now put an end to this affair, and if poffible, forget it for ever.

If it will not be too painful to you my lord, I would intreat you, with thefe gentlemen our friends, to follow me into the eaft apartment, the fcene of my parents woes, and yet the dawning of my better hopes.

They rofe to attend him, he committed the lady Emma to the care of her youngeft brother, obferving that the fcene was too folemn for a lady to be prefent.—they proceeded to the apartment, he fhewed the baron the fatal clofet, and the place where the bones were found, alfo the trunk that contained them.—he reca- pitulated all that paffed before their arrival.— he fhewed them the coffin where the bones of the unfortunate pair were depofited.—he then
desired

defired the baron to give orders for their inter-.
ment.—no, faid he, it belongs to you to order,
and every one here is ready to perform it.——
Edmund then defired father Oiwald to give
notice to the friars of the monaftry of it. Auftin,
that, with their permiffion, the funeral fhould
be folemnized there, and the bones interred in
the church ; he alfo gave orders that the clofet fhould be floored, the apartment repaired,
and put in order.—he then returned to the
other fide of the caftle.

Preparations being made for the funeral, it
was performed a few days after.—Edmund attended in perfon as chief mourner, fir Philip
Harclay as the fecond; Jofeph defired he might
affift as fervant to the deceafed.—they were
followed by moft people of the village.—the
ftory was now become publick, and every one
bleffed Edmund for the piety and devotion with
which he performed the laft duties to his parents.—Edmund appeared in deep mourning
the week after ; he affifted at a mafs for the
repofe of the deceafed

Sir Philip Harclay ordered a monument to
be erected to the memory of his friends, with
the following infcription.

" Praye for the foules of Authur lord Lovele
" and Marie his wife who were cutt off in the
" flowere of theire youthe, bye the trecherye
" and crueltie of theire neare kinnefmanne.—
" Edmunde theire onlie fonne, one and twentie
" yeares after their deathe, by the direction
" of heavene, made the difcoverye of the man-
" nere of theire deathe, and at the fame time
" proved his owne birthe.—he collected theire
" bones together, and interred them in this
" place.

" place.—a warning and proofe to late pof-
" teritie, of the juitice of providence, and the
" certaintie of Retribution."

The Sunday after the funeral, Edmund
threw off his mourning, and appeared in a drefs
fuitable to his condition.——he received the
compliments of his friends with eafe and chearfulnefs, and began to enjoy his happinefs.—
he afked an audience of his fair miftrefs, and
was permitted to declare the paffion he had
fo long ftiffled in his own bofom —fhe gave
him a favourable hearing, and in a fhort time
confeffed that fhe had fuffered equally in the
fufpenfe that was fo grievous to him.—they
engaged themfelves by mutual vows to each
other, and only waited the baron's pleafure
to complete their happinefs; every cloud was
vanifhed from their brows, and fweet tranquility took poffeffion of their bofoms.—their
friends fhared their happinefs, William and
Edmund renewed their vows of everlafting
friendfhip, and promifed to be as much together as William's other duties would permit.

The baron once more fummoned all his
company together; he told Edmund all that
paffed relating to his brother-in-law, his exile
and the pilgrimage of Zadifky; he then related the circumftances of fir Robert's engagement to lord Clifford's daughter, his eftablifhment in his uncle's feat, and his own obligations to return time enough to be prefent at
the marriage; but before I go, faid he, I will
give my daughter to the heir of Lovel, and
then I fhall have difcharged my duty to him,
and my promife to fir Philip Harclay.

You

You have nobly performed both, said fir Philip, and whenever you depart I fhall be your companion.—what, faid Edmund, am I to be deprived of both my fathers at once ?—my honoured lord, you have given away two houfes, where do you intend to refide ?—no matter, faid the baron, I know I fhall be welcome to both.—my dear lord, faid Edmund, ftay here and be ftill the mafter, I fhall be proud to be under your command, and to be your fervant as well as your fon !—no Edmund, faid the baron, that would not now be proper, this is your caftle, you are its lord and mafter, and it is incumbent on you to fhow yourfelf worthy of the great things providence has done for you.—how fhall I, a young man, acquit myfelf of fo many duties as will be upon me, without the advice and affiftance of my two paternal friends? oh fir Philip, will you too leave me? once you gave me hopes.—he ftopped, greatly affected.—fir Philip faid, tell me truly, Edmund, do you really defire that I fhould live with you ?—as truly fir, as I defire life and happinefs !——then my dear child, I will live and die with you !—they embraced with tears of affection, and Edmund was all joy and gratitude.—my good lord, faid fir Philip, you have difpofed of two houfes, and have none ready to receive you, will you accept of mine, it is much at your fervice, and its being in the fame county with your eldeft fon, will be an inducement to you to refide there ?—the baron caught fir Philip's hand.—noble fir, I thank you, and I will embrace your kind offer, I will be your tenant for the prefent, my caftle in Wales fhall be put in repair,

in the mean time, if I do not reside there, it
will be an eftablifhment for one of my younger
fons; but what will you do with your old ſol-
diers and dependants?—my lord, I will never
caſt them off, there is another houſe on my
eſtate that has been ſhut up many years, I will
have it repaired and furniſhed properly for the
reception of my old men; I will endow it with
a certain ſum to be paid annually, and I will
appoint a ſteward to manage their revenue; I
will continue it during the lives of the firſt in-
habitants, and after that I ſhall leave it to my
fon here, to do as he pleaſes.—your ſon, ſaid
Edmund, will make it the buſineſs of his life
to act worthy of ſuch a father.—enough, ſaid
fir Philip, I am ſatisfied that you will; I purpofe to reſide myſelf in that very apartment
which my dear friend your father inhabited;
I will tread in his footſteps, and think he ſees
me acting his part in his ſon's family; I will
be attended by my own ſervants, and whenever you deſire it, I will give you my company; your joys, your griefs ſhall be mine, I
ſhall hold your children in my arms, and their
prattle ſhall amuſe my old age; and as my
laſt earthly wiſh, your hands ſhall cloſe my
eyes.—long, very long, ſaid Edmund, (with
eyes and hands lifted up) may it be e'er I perform fo fad a duty!—long and happily may
you live together, ſaid the baron, I will hope
to fee you fometimes, and to claim a ſhare in
your bleſſings!—but let us give no more tears
to ſorrow, the reſt ſhall be thoſe of joy and
tranſport; the firſt ſtep we take ſhall be to
marry our Edmund, I will give orders for the
celebration, and they ſhall be the laſt orders I
ſhall

fhall give in this houfe.—they then feparated and went to prepare for the approaching folemnity.

Sir Philip and the baron had a private conference concerning Edmund's affuming the name and title of Lovel.—I am refolved, faid fir Philip, to go to the king, to acquaint him briefly with Edmund's hiftory; I will requeft that he may be called up to parliament by a writ, for there is no need of a new patent, he being the true inheritor; in the mean time he fhall affume the name, arms and title, and I will anfwer any one that fhall difpute his right to them.—fir Philip then declared his refolution to fet out with the baron at his departure, and to fettle all his other affairs before he returned to take up his refidence at the caftle.

A few days after, the marriage was celebrated to the entire fatisfaction of all parties. —the baron ordered the doors to be thrown open, and the houfe free for all comers, with every other token of joy and feftivity.—Edmund appeared full of joy without levity, of mirth without extravagance.—he received the congratulations of his friends, with eafe, freedom and vivacity; he fent for his fofter father, and mother, who began to think themfelves neglected, as he had been fo deeply engaged in affairs of more confequence, that he had not been particularly attentive to them; he made them come into the great hall, and prefented them to his lady.

Thefe, faid he, are the good people to whom I am, under God, indebted for my prefent happinefs; they were my firft benefactors,

I was

I was obliged to them for food and suftenance in my childhood, and this good woman nourifhed my infancy at her own breaft.—the lady received them gracioufly, and faluted Margery. —Andrew kneeled down, and with great humility, begged Edmund's pardon for his treatment of him in his childhood.—I heartily forgive you, faid he, and I will excufe you to yourfelf; it was natural for you to look upon me as an intruder, that was eating your children's bread; you faved my life, and afterwards you fuftained it by your food and raiment? I ought to have maintained myfelf, and to have contributed to your maintenance; but befides this, your treatment of me was the firft of my preferment, it recommended me to the notice of this noble family; every thing that happened to me fince, has been a ftep to my prefent ftate of honour and happinefs; never man had fo many benefactors as myfelf, but both they and myfelf have been only inftruments in the hands of providence, to bring about its own purpofes; let us praife God for all! I fhared your poverty, and you fhall fhare my riches; I will give you the cottage where you dwell, and the ground about it; I will alfo pay you the annual fum of ten pounds for the lives of you both, I will put out your children to manual trades, and affift you to provide for them in their own ftation, and you are to look upon this as paying a debt, and not beftowing a gift; I owe you more than I can ever pay, and if there be any thing further in my power that will contribute to your happinefs, you can afk nothing in reafon that I will deny you.

Andrew

Andrew hid his face.—I cannot bear it! said he, oh what a brute was I, to abuse such a child as this! I shall never forgive myself!— you must indeed my friend, for I forgive and thank you!—Andrew retired back, but Margery came forward, she looked earnestly on Edmund, she then threw her arms about his neck, and wept aloud.—my precious child! my lovely babe, thank God I have lived to see this day!—I will rejoice in your good fortune, and your bounty to us, but I must ask one more favour yet? that I may sometimes come hither and behold that gracious countenance, and thank God that I was honoured so far as to give thee food from my own breast, and to bring thee up to be a blessing to me, and to all that know thee?—Edmund was affected, he returned her embrace; he bad her come to the castle as often as she pleased, and she should always be received as his mother; the bride saluted her, and told her the oftener she came, the more welcome she should be.—Margery and her husband retired full of blessings and prayers for their happiness.—she gave vent to her joy, by relating to the servants and neighbours every circumstance of Edmund's birth, infancy and childhood.—many a tear was dropped by the auditors, and many a prayer wafted to heaven for his happiness.—Joseph took up the story where she left it; he told the rising dawn of youth and virtue, darting its rays through the clouds of obscurity, and how every stroke of envy and malignity brushed away some part of the darkness that veiled its lustre: he told the story of the haunted apartment, and all the conse-

R 3   quences

quences of it, how he and Ofwald conveyed the youth away from the caftle, no more to return till he came as mafter of it.—he clofed the tale with praife to heaven for the happy difcovery, that gave fuch an heir to the houfe of Lovel ; to his dependants fuch a lord and mafter ; to mankind a friend and benefactor.— there was truly a houfe of joy, not that falfe kind, in the midft of which there is heavinefs, but that of rational creatures, grateful to the fupreme benefactor, raifing their minds by a due enjoyment of earthly bleffings, to a prepa- ration for a more perfect ftate hereafter.

A few days after the wedding, the lord Fitz Owen began to prepare for his journey to the north.—he gave to Edmund the plate, linen, and furniture of the caftle, the farming ftock and utenfils ; he would have added a fum of money, but fir Philip ftopped his hand.— we do not forget, faid he, that you have other children, we will not fuffer you to injure them ; give us your bleffing and paternal af- fection, and we have nothing more to afk : I told you my lord, that you and I fhould one day be fincere friends.—we muft be fo, an- fwered the baron, it is impoffible to be long your enemy, we are brothers, and fhall be to our lives end.

They regulated the young man's houfehold, the baron gave leave to the fervants to choofe their mafter.—the elder ones followed him, (except Jofeph, who defired to live with Edmund, as the chief happinefs of his life.) moft of the younger ones chofe the fervice of the youthful pair.—there was a tender and affectionate parting on all fides.—Edmund be- fought

fought his beloved William not to leave him.
—the baron faid, he muft infift on his being
at his brother's wedding, as a due attention
to him, but after that he fhould return to the
caftle for fome time.

The baron and fir Philip Harclay, and their
train fet forward.—fir Philip went to London
and obtained all he defired for his Edmund;
from thence he went into Yorkfhire, and fettled his affairs there, removing his penfioners
to his other houfe, and putting lord Fitz-Owen
in poffeffion of his own; they had a generous
contention about the terms, but fir Philip infifted on the baron's accepting the ufe of every
thing there, you hold it in truft for a future
grandchild, faid he, whom I hope to live to
endow with it.

During fir Philip's abfence, the young lord
Lovel caufed the haunted apartment to be repaired and turnifhed for the reception of his father by adoption.—he placed his friend Jofeph
over all his men fervants, and ordered him to
forbear his attendance, but the old man would
always ftand at the fide board, and feaft his
eyes with the countenance of his own mafter's
fon, furrounded with honour and happinefs.—
John Wyatt waited upon the perfon of his
lord, and enjoyed his favour without abate-
ment.——mr. William Fitz-Owen accompanied fir Philip Harclay from the north country, when he returned to take up his refidence
at the caftle of Lovel.

Edmund in the arms of love and friendfhip,
enjoyed with true relifh the bleffings that furrounded him, with an heart overflowing with
benevolence to his fellow creatures, and raptures

tures of gratitude to his Creator.—his lady and himself were examples of conjugal affection and happiness.—within a year from his marriage she brought him a son and heir, whose birth renewed the joy and congratulations of all his friends.—the baron Fitz-Owen came to the baptism, and partook of his children's blessings; the child was called Arthur, after the name of his grandfather.

The year following was born a second son, who was called Philip Harclay, upon him the noble knight of that name settled his estate in Yorkshire; and by the king's permission, he took the name and arms of that family.

The third son was called William, he inherited the fortune of his uncle of that name, who adopted him, and he made the castle of Lovel his residence, and died a bachelor.

The fourth son was called Edmund, the fifth Owen, and there was also a daughter called Emma.

When time had worn out the prejudices of sir Robert Fitz-Owen, the good old baron of that name, proposed a marriage between his eldest son and heir, and the daughter of Edmund lord Lovel, which was happily concluded.—the nuptials were honoured with the presence of both families, and the old baron was so elevated with this happy union of his descendants, that he cried out.—now I am ready to die, I have lived long enough! this is the band of love that unites all my children to me, and to each other!—he did not long survive this happy event, he died full of years and honours, and his name was never mentioned but with the deepest marks of gratitude,

love

love and veneration·—sweet is the remembrance of the virtuous, and happy are the descendants of such a father! they will think on him and emulate his virtues, they will remember him, and be ashamed to degenerate from their ancestor.

Many years after sir Philip Harclay settled at the castle, he received tidings from his friend Zaditky, by one of the two servants who attended him to the holy land.—from him he learned that his friend had discovered by private advices, that he had a son living in Palestine, which was the chief motive of his leaving England.—that he met with various adventures in pertuit of him ; that at length he found him, converted him to the chriftian religion, and then persuaded him to retire from the world into a monaftry by the fide of mount Libanus, where he intended to end his days.

That Walter, commonly called lord Lovel, had entered into the fervice of the Greek emperor, John Paleologus, not bearing to undergo a life of folitude aud retirement.—that he made up a ftory of his being compelled to leave his native country by his relations, for having accidentially killed one of them, and that he was treated with great cruelty and injuftice, that he had accepted a poft in the emperor's army, and was foon after married to the daughter of one of the chief officers of it.

Zadifly forefaw, and lamented the downfal of that empire, and withdrew from the ftorm he faw approaching.—finally he bad the meffenger tell fir Philip Harclay and his adopted fon, that he fhould not ceafe to pray for them, and defired their prayers in return.

Sir Philip defired lord Lovel to entertain this meffenger in his fervice.—that good knight lived to extreme old age in honour and happinefs, and died in the arms of his beloved Edmund, who alfo performed the laft duties to his faithful Jofeph.

Father Ofwald lived many years in the family as chaplain, he retired from thence at length, and died in his own monaftry.

Edmund lord Lovel lived to old age, in peace, honour and happinefs, and died in the arms of his children.

Sir Philip Harclay caufed the papers relating to his fon's hiftory to be collected together, the firft part of it was written under his own eye in Yorkfhire, the fubfequent parts by father Ofwald at the caftle of Lovel.—all thefe when together, furnifh a ftriking leffon to pofterity, of the over-ruling hand of providence, and the certainty of RETRIBUTION.

F I N I S.

LaVergne, TN USA
15 March 2011
220229LV00002B/187/P

9 781165 777105